PREGNANCY *for the* SKEPTICAL *Woman*

A Practical Guide and Memoir

SADIE LAURENS

ISBN 978-1-955156-35-6 (paperback)
ISBN 978-1-955156-36-3 (digital)

Copyright © 2021 by Sadie Laurens

All rights reserved. No part of this publication may be reproduced, distributed, or transmitted in any form or by any means, including photocopying, recording, or other electronic or mechanical methods without the prior written permission of the publisher. For permission requests, solicit the publisher via the address below.

Rushmore Press LLC
1 800 460 9188
www.rushmorepress.com

Printed in the United States of America

CONTENTS

Introduction v

1	Pregnancy for the Skeptical Woman	1
2	What Kind of Pregnant Woman Do You Want to Be?	4
3	It Started off Skeptically	8
4	We're Not Out of the Woods Yet	11
5	Genetic Counseling and the First Trimester Screening	14
6	Getting There Is Half the Battle	17
7	Maternity Clothes	21
8	Why Is It Called Morning Sickness?	27
9	Baby Gear	29
10	The Baby Registry	30
11	A Reflection on Baby Gear	33
12	Breastfeeding	38
13	Whose Breasts Are These?	40
14	Breast Health	42
15	A Reflection on Breasts	43
16	Cravings—It's Not Just Pickles and Ice Cream	46
17	The Ultrasound and the Second Trimester Screening	48
18	Kids, Not Clones	54
19	Baby Nightmares: Quick, Before I forget!	56
20	Pre Baby Preparation	58
21	A Reflection on Pre Baby Preparation	60
22	Prenatal Pampering and Self-Care	62
23	Taking Time for Yourself	64
24	Freakish Body Changes	65

25	Support	69
26	The Glucose Tolerance Test	73
27	Please, Don't Tell Me to Relax	75
28	Ten Weeks and Counting Down	77
29	Maternity Leave	80
30	A Reflection on Maternity Leave	81
31	Strange Baby Questions	83
32	The Baby Shower	85
33	Packing for the Hospital	87
34	A Reflection on Packing for the Hospital	89
35	Cord Blood Banking	91
36	The Countdown	93
37	The Game Plan	94
38	Giving Birth	96
39	So You've Missed Your Due Date	98
40	After You Give Birth	100
41	I'm Not Depressed—I'm Stressed	104
42	Parenting for the Skeptical Woman: The First Ten Years	106

References 109

INTRODUCTION

Why *Pregnancy for the Skeptical Woman*?

I knew I wanted to have children. I also knew that I have never been able to go with the flow. I need planning and preparation. I need to hear the bad before the good. I weigh my options, opportunities, and life choices. I am neither trusting nor romantic. I have not had a life that has taught me any other way than to approach each opportunity and challenge with fierce responsibility, a firm knowledge base, and pragmatism.

My early research into trying to conceive and become pregnant quickly taught me that I was going to need a lot of patience to wade through the gushy, passive, and sugarcoated crap that disguises itself as information for pregnant women. I didn't want war stories; I wanted a fair and balanced look at pregnancy—the daily or weekly experiences that most pregnant women have to face. I need a community of voices if I am going to learn about this pregnancy thing. As I did this, I kept track of my own experiences that allowed me to throw my hat in that ring and form my own "pregnancy mom" voice.

I found little out there that resonated with me. At the time I became pregnant I was four months into the blog, *Two Man Minimum*, where I chronicled my approach to my present life coming from an ill-prepared matriarchal childhood. No pun intended, but it was here that *Pregnancy for the Skeptical Woman* was born. Because what am I if not a skeptical woman?

Being a skeptic does not mean that I am a pessimistic naysayer. It simply means that I need to research and make an informed decision on my own about every situation I encounter. From romance to pregnancy, I'm not going to take anyone's word for it—unless they are brutally honest and have done their homework.

So here is the brutally honest experience of my first pregnancy.

1

Pregnancy for the Skeptical Woman

I have never considered myself very maternal, but I have always wanted to have kids. Since I was a teenager I noticed that animals and babies like me so hopefully this means that I am a pretty good person and not giving off a crazy vibe to the vulnerable.

Five years ago I started dating my second husband. He was in the midst of a hideous divorce where his main concern was his two children and his ex's main concern was how much money she could milk out of the situation. When we started dating I knew that this was potential stepmom territory so there were immediately other people involved in this relationship who would be affected by this relationship.

I have step-parents, as does my husband, so the situation was nothing new, but before I knew it, I was a full-time stepmom with a three-year-old and five-year-old and that's when I realized just how different my life would be. The big joke between my husband and I is that I was a parent before I became a mother.

Gone were the twelve-hour workdays where I would come home and hang out with my dogs. Now I had other people to consider in my schedule: I had to shop differently, speak differently, and get used to gross things that I never thought I would do.

All of a sudden I needed to buy more than yogurt, coffee, and pretzels. I had to buy things like pull-ups, sippy cups, Baby Goldfish, and Cheerios. Cursing was out the window, and my Mustang convertible was suddenly a family vehicle. I felt like I had all these sacrifices to make. I wasn't unwilling. I was young. I was adapting.

Jamie and I were a couple every other weekend but a family of four five days a week. And then there is always the ex-wife lurking and doing her damage to sabotage any ounce of nurturing progress Jamie and I made as a family. After a divorce, when mommy has a boyfriend, that's okay. When daddy has a girlfriend, she's a whore. The double standard could not be further from the truth and it is as frustrating now as it was then.

The name-calling, the labels, the stereotypes—it's easy to get caught up in them. I was more caught up with the reality that I went from being an only child to being in a blended family with two children. I went from no baby experience to having a three-year-old puke on me. It seemed like my life skipped a step.

A year after we were married, we bought a house. That's when the change happened. Suddenly the idea of moving beyond being a stepmom to just being a mom started to work its way into my consciousness.

I used to look at babies and if I didn't make them cry I was happy with that. If I could make one laugh, great. I never really thought about having one. I knew I wanted to, but going from "wanted to" to "want to try" is a life-altering moment. I had the moment. I felt like I unpacked the feeling when we moved into our house. But I was not going to admit it—not yet, no way. I had to come to terms with it on my own first. Regardless of the fact that Jamie and I both knew we wanted kids, he always said to "let him know when."

Okay. How? Do I send a card? An e-mail? Do I update my Facebook status? Twitter, perhaps? Oh, no, better—I'll write a blog because that's not public at all, is it?

It was during the first Halloween in our new house. I dressed up like a witch, decked out my yard, and distributed candy out of a bubbling cauldron to the neighborhood children. And with every baby ladybug or pumpkin wheeled up to my Dutch door in a stroller who trustingly grabbed the candy from my hand this feeling got stronger. It was the tick, tick, tick of my biological clock. I wasn't going to give in to it that quickly. I'm not crazy. No, I gave him a warning.

On Halloween, dressed as a witch, I said, "So, yeah, honey, not now, but this time next year, if we could be pregnant or trying, that would be good for me. What do you think?"

His answer?

"Okay."

That's it?

That was my slick way of breaking the news. Did he not know how significant this was? Did he not know what I was giving up? Those free alternate weekends for a baby who will never leave? Did he understand the shift that this was for me?

I first got my period when I was eleven. From that moment, my mother said, "It means that you can have babies, but you won't for a very long time, will you?" I have spent the last twenty-one years *not* getting pregnant. I have been very successful. In fact, I play awesome defense. I start doing "age math" in my brain.

Sadie, you're thirty-two, you're three years away from being a high-risk pregnancy, my brain would tell me. *As it is, with any luck, you'll be forty-three with a ten-year-old. Fifty-three with a twenty-year-old, but Jamie is four years older than you.*

Time became the enemy. What if all those years of not getting pregnant was only because you're possibly infertile? Then what?

We start dieting; exercising; and eating better, making up for those years of tequila, coffee, cigarettes, nonorganic meat, midnight grilled cheese, Burger King, and weight gain. At that moment, I felt like I was training for a marathon, one that—if I'm lucky—I'll qualify for.

Then I made a mistake. I googled "pregnancy" only to learn terms like "trying to conceive," "cervical mucus," and "basal body temperature." I found lists of things to do and not do, other websites to consult and books to read, cycles to track.

Now I am terrified. What if my days of "awesome defense" is really just infertility? What if I never get the chance for another three-year-old to puke on me again? What if I don't get to buy Baby Goldfish or little shoes ever again?

What happened to the overacademic workaholic? Where did she go? How will all of this end?

Next month, we take our marks on the starting line.

2

What Kind of Pregnant Woman Do You Want to Be?

If you found this book because you are planning to conceive, your pregnancy emotions may be running high by now. You may find that you are frequently impatient, irritable, or completely self-involved and perhaps you think there is nothing wrong with feeling like the world should bow to you because you will soon be pregnant.

Perhaps you are caught by the web of social media that is ladened with birth announcements or Insta posts of babies wrapped in burlap sitting in a wooden crate. It's a thing. It's supposed to be cute, but that line just read like something from a crime scene.

As excited as you may be, please come down to earth. The planet does not owe you anything for procreating. You are a hormonal fountain; please refrain from spraying innocent bystanders. Take frequent breaks not from being pregnant but from the social emotional tornado that it can create. Remember, there might be people around you who are struggling to conceive or who want to create a family through nontraditional means. So if you are an able-bodied woman having a baby you can celebrate, just remember, this isn't really anything groundbreaking. It's new to you. Celebrate that, but stay tethered to earth. Take a moment to recognize your privilege. Reset your mind. Be kind to others.

Pregnancy is a very unique time in your life. There are few times when people are so focused and interested in how you are feeling and what is going on in the mystical world that has become your body.

The truth is, you are not alone. You did not invent the womb or the ability to procreate. It's okay to be excited and maybe a little self-involved, but please do not go off the deep end. It's really not about you; it's about the baby, which happens to be inside of you. Try not to act like a pregnancy diva.

What do I mean? Perhaps you think I sound like a bitch right now. Well, there are different types of pregnant women—there are women who need the opinion of everybody she knows in order to make a single decision and there are personality types who take great comfort in getting multiple opinions. My point here is this: when you get pregnant, everyone will try to give you their opinions and advice. Sometimes it comes from a place of nostalgia. Keep reflecting on this throughout your pregnancy. It may change, it may change from pregnancy to pregnancy.

The beauty of listening to others is that if you put ten mothers in a room to share the journey into motherhood, you will walk away with ten very different stories.

It's best to reflect how much input you want. I have seen perfectly rational women get pregnant and go off the fucking deep end.

Take Mary, for example. Many years ago, Mary was my next-door neighbor. She was an accomplished businesswoman. She and her husband decided to get pregnant. Mary snapped from the moment she started trying to get pregnant. One day, at a barbecue, someone was sitting next to her drinking a margarita and smoking a cigarette. Mary jumps up and exclaims, "I can't be around this!"

Two months later, she got pregnant; and with every month, Mary turned into a complete self-involved, holier-than-thou nightmare. Mary was the woman who told everyone—from her mother to the mail carrier—that she was pregnant the day the stick had a positive result. No sensible waiting period for her.

When Mary was about four months pregnant, I came home from work at the same time she did. I said, "Hi, Mary, how are you?"

"Well, I had my minimuffins that I keep in the office as a snack, but I didn't have my milk today," she replied.

"Okay, well, I'll see you later."

I had nothing to say, but I heard horror movie music in my head as I walked away.

Another day, when Mary was about six months pregnant, she received a speeding ticket. It was a Saturday afternoon. I was walking to my car as she was walking into her house, clutching the speeding ticket and looking distraught.

"Hi, Mary, is everything okay?" I asked.

"No, I got a speeding ticket on my way home from the mall. I have a life growing inside me, I shouldn't have to deal with this."

"That's too bad. Okay, well, I'll see you later."

And I made a mental note to refill my oral contraceptive.

This was a good eight years before I ever considered having a baby, but it was a bone-chilling moment nonetheless. Where the fuck did Mary go? Who was this milk-guzzling, self-centered zombie in her place?

Mary gave birth and never returned. Her life became about the fact that she was a mother. She can't go out because she's a mother. She can't say this or that because she is a mother.

Your life is going to change, no matter what. You are going to change. You can't go through the experience of getting pregnant, being pregnant, being responsible for another human, and expect to be the same person you were before the journey.

I think what many accomplished women fear is losing the drive that made them successful. I like to think of it this way: if you can have the drive to be a successful woman in the twenty-first century—one of the most competitive and stressful centuries for a woman—then you can have the strength to be you and be a mother. You are you, but your life is enriched. Even if you are tired and stressed out. Even if you are freaked out beyond belief. Be an enriched you, not the pompous, off-the-deep-end you. Remember, recognize and reset, and then ask yourself, *What kind of pregnant woman do I want to be?*

Well, as soon as I decided that I wanted to have a baby, I needed to reel myself in. Suddenly, I remembered Mary and every other psycho mother I have ever seen in a supermarket. Sometimes it felt like I was watching a zombie apocalypse. Maybe women freak out after pregnancy because they don't have enough support for themselves and the baby. Maybe there is the need to keep up.

I don't want to be the "I am more important than you" variety.

I do not want to be the one who is constantly cooed at and stroking her belly in a "sacred vessel" sort of way.

I don't want to be the "I'm eating for two" woman—let's just say the universe mocked me for that. I ate for a football team.

I will *not* be a "Mother Earth natural" woman. I am not turning my nose up at drugs; I will neither give birth at home or in a bathtub. I will remind myself that this process is nothing new—it's just new to me. I will recognize and reset.

3

It Started off Skeptically

I consider myself a rather intelligent woman. So when I learned that I had no idea about trying to conceive, I was surprised. We started trying in August. I refused to use the TTC abbreviation that is so popular on the baby-planning websites. The terminology of sites like The Bump and BabyCenter make me want to gag. There's "baby dancing" (eww), there's DH (dear husband)—how wrought with patriarchy and cisgender is that?—and then there's TTC, or "trying to conceive." Jamie and I opted for "trying." This term worked on two levels. We're *trying* to get pregnant and we are no longer *trying* to prevent it. It seemed tastefully vague.

Trying is packed with codes between partners to update the baby-making status. It seems like an attempt to emotionally distance yourself from the situation. There's a lot of rejection in knowing that you "missed the landing" in a particular month. It's easy to feel like your body is failing you. The baby-making websites will tell you to take a "babymoon"—i.e., a vacation dedicated to procreating.

However, I find vacationing extremely stressful. It throws off my entire system. I can't sleep on vacation, I can't even poop on vacation, and now I'm supposed to get pregnant?

I schedule a preconception check up with my ob-gyn. She tells me to try every other day and, if we are not successful, to come back in nine months. So far, I know that I have to look for signs of ovulation—the days usually about two weeks before your period—and then call in the swimmers. Getting pregnant is about timing, and that made me nervous. We needed a system. We created an original plan, and every month when we were unsuccessful, we would bring in additional conception methods.

During the first month, we relied on the counting the days until ovulation and prenatal vitamins. The second month, we counted the days and used an ovulation prediction kit. The third month, I started drinking whole fat milk instead of skim on the theory that additional hormones in whole fat milk aid fertility. It's gross—and ten years later, I'm vegan—but I can't say for sure that it didn't help. We continued with the vitamins and the ovulation prediction kit. Each unsuccessful month brought more anxiety. Of course, every website will tell you not to get stressed out when trying because this alone can impede fertility. Every month, I could not help but think, *How does this process not cause stress?*

Over the next two months, I would literally piss away close to sixty dollars on pregnancy tests. I did not understand the travel time necessary for a fertilized egg to implant. I thought you had sex and *poof*—you were pregnant. I never realized that the egg had to travel through the fallopian tubes, to the uterus, and implant. One night, Jamie and I tried. Literally the next morning, I took a test. Naturally, I was crestfallen when I told him that afternoon that we "missed the landing."

"Why did you waste a test?" he asked.

"What do you mean? Aren't you disappointed?" I replied.

"Umm, no. There's no way that egg was fertilized, traveled to your uterus, and already implanted. You actually just *pissed* away fifteen dollars," he explained.

I forgot the most basic elements of female reproduction. I had to face the fact that biology did not care about how impatient I was.

During the third month, Jamie was diagnosed with an abdominal hernia and needed to have surgery in the second week of the month, also known as "the trying week." I figured all bets were off. There was no way we could nail the landing that month. There was too much against us. Jamie insisted we keep going. Because when does a guy ever turn down sex? Sure enough, we nailed the landing.

As I said earlier, I literally pissed away close to sixty dollars' worth of tests before I admitted it to Jamie. These were the really good name-brand tests. On November 4, my period barely one week late, I used the last test in my arsenal. I was down to one backup test from the dollar store.

Again, I did everything wrong. There I was, barely a week late, it was 11:00 a.m. in the morning, not even the first specimen of the day, and I'm taking a dollar-store pregnancy test. I look at it—of course, there's no line. I put the test on the bathroom counter and wash my face. I reach down to pick up the test, and I think I see a pink line. However, my bathroom lighting felt like it was playing tricks on me.

Quickly I rummage through the trash for the box. How long has it been? I read the directions on the box (I realize, for the first time ever): "For best results, read the test after three minutes but not after ten minutes." Hmmm, maybe a more expensive test buys you clearer directions, but I'll take what I can get right now.

I carefully walk into the bedroom; I need a second opinion. I wake up Jamie.

"Can you look at something for me?" I ask. "Do you see a line?"

I know I am about to be reprimanded for my impatience. But as a good sport, he holds the test under the nightstand lamp.

"There's a line," he says and rolls over to go back to sleep.

Now there was no magical moment here. He didn't pick me up and spin me around or rub my stomach. Just thinking about a scenario like that makes me gag. Seriously, I can't tell you how many people asked me about "the moment I told him." As if, what? He didn't know it was coming? No, none of the clichés. This is real life, not *Guiding Light*.

Ten years later, social media has encouraged making such a big deal out of revealing to a father that a baby is coming; I can't get behind that. There was some relief that we were at the end of a stressful project. If nothing else, we had some reassurance that we were not infertile. Baby making was over.

4

We're Not Out of the Woods Yet

The day after my positive test result, I called my ob-gyn's office. They walk me through a short series of questions, the date of my last menstrual cycle (which I learned will become as important a date as my social security number), and they schedule me for a six-week visit.

Jamie, who has decided to come to every doctor's appointment with me, and I go in for the ultrasound. Now, had I not googled the term "six week ultrasound" (www.baby2see.com), I would have been totally unprepared for a vaginal ultrasound (www.pregnancy.org). Not that it's a big deal, but I had always thought of ultrasounds as external procedures; to be probed internally in front of your husband may be a bit uncomfortable. The ob-gyn has always been a very personal doctor's visit. There's a moment of adjustment when you put on a paper dress in front of your spouse. Let's not even talk about the stirrups.

At the appointment, I go in first. The nurse checks my vitals, gives me a gown, and I wait for the doctor. She and I decide to do the scan first and then call in Jamie. I was very relieved by the fact that you're not really probed. It's more of a just-the-tip situation. It's not nearly as bad as it sounds.

Now, here's the moment I'm waiting for, right? The big fetus unveiling. Shouldn't there be a little heartbeat flicker? Some Tic Tac–sized creature waving at me? There's nothing. There is a little circle—a sac, as my doctor calls it. I am totally confused.

Noticing my confusion, my doctor starts to ask me some questions in order to figure out what we are seeing. The big question here is, is this just an empty gestational sac or is there some microscopic bunch of cells in there?

"What was the date of your last period?" she asks.

"October 4," I say.

"Have you had any spotting?"

"Just a little, yesterday." I was about to bring this up when she beat me to it.

"How long is your cycle usually?"

"My cycle? Oh, it's long, I say. About every thirty-five days."

"Then this means you're not at six weeks. You're closer to four or five. Spotting may have actually been implantation. This is exactly what I should be seeing."

Not to leave anything to chance, she immediately sends me for bloodwork. Three hours later, she calls me to let me know that everything is normal. All of the hormone levels are high, which means that somewhere in that sac, something is growing.

Let's return to the topic of timing. Everything you will read on the internet about "TTC" is usually based on a twenty-eight-day menstrual cycle. So if you are like me, you really need to look for signs of ovulation rather than just count the days. Also, if my entire cycle is extended, this probably means that when we first started trying, we may have started too late or stopped trying too soon. Bringing in the ovulation prediction kit was definitely a good idea. Secondarily, that last resort—the dollar-store pregnancy test—predicted a pregnancy that was barely starting. That's pretty damn good for a buck.

My doctor scheduled me to come back three weeks later for a rescan. Three weeks later in the darkened examining room, in another paper dress (one of many), Jamie and I see a tiny, little, rice-sized creature and a flicker. You'll see the heartbeat first. It will be a few more weeks until you are able to hear it.

However, according to www.medhelp.com, once you see the heartbeat, the rate of miscarriage drops about 5 percent. The miscarriage rate will drop again after you hear the heartbeat at twelve weeks. But I'm a skeptic, remember? As far as I'm concerned, there is no baby. That's right. I'm a skeptic. I'm pro-choice, and none of that is changing just because I am "with fetus." My doctor's philosophy is "the more symptoms, the better." Until about twenty weeks, there's no guarantee.

At this eight-week rescan, my doctor gingerly suggests the recommended "first trimester screening." She says it in such a soft, almost breathy manner, as to not spark the religious or political convictions of her patients. I can tell by her delivery that this suggestion is not always well received. I quickly relieve her trepidation, "Sure, where do I make the appointment?"

Let's talk about miscarriages. That's right, I said the "m-word." And if you are pregnant or planning on becoming pregnant (otherwise, why else would you be reading this book unless you are related to me?), you better get used to that word too because there is a strong miscarriage undercurrent for the first twelve to fifteen weeks of pregnancy, if not longer.

During the first twelve weeks of pregnancy, miscarriage sounds like a dirty word. But consider what (more honest) baby websites tell you. Many miscarriages are due to chromosomal abnormalities within the fetus that will inhibit its ability to thrive. As difficult as it may seem, don't get too attached in the first twenty weeks.

Miscarriages are devastating. Women, couples, partners share their stories of loss because they need to heal from the grief. No one walks around with a sign saying they just miscarried. A few pages ago we talked about being sensitive to others; this applies here.

The general rule of thumb is to hold off on announcing your pregnancy until you are twelve weeks pregnant. If you are really against having a special-needs baby, you might want to curb your excitement until the spina bifida test around week 20.

5

Genetic Counseling and the First Trimester Screening

Being with a fetus is both exciting and terrifying. The excitement is based on the hope that everything is developing normally. The terror comes from the possibility that everything will suddenly end with a miscarriage or that you will get terrifying news during the first trimester screening.

No matter what happens, fetuses can fail to develop because there is something that will prevent them from thriving after birth. It can feel tragic; it is nature. It's terrifying. How do you not get attached to the fetus? How do you not fall into a pregnancy pattern of getting used to your body and hormones even after a few short weeks? After trying to conceive and finally getting pregnant, it's easy to think *baby* and not *fetus*. I just kept telling myself not to get my hopes up. Meanwhile, I was thinking about baby names.

Jamie and I decided that we will tell everyone the once we get through the first trimester screening, which we were scheduled for at thirteen weeks of gestation. Conveniently, our appointment was for the morning of December 31, 2009—10:20 a.m., to be exact.

This test occurs at a genetic counselor's office. It requires a series of bloodwork, a painfully full bladder, and a high-definition ultrasound that determines the risk of Down syndrome and other more serious chromosomal issues that can keep the fetus from thriving. The genetic counselor is there to talk you in from the ledge if you get bad news.

The FTS (first trimester screening) begins with a series of bloodwork that is taken about a week before the scan. These tests must occur between twelve and thirteen weeks of gestation. For the FTS, I had to drink twenty-five ounces of water thirty minutes before the test. The nurse with whom I made my appointment made sure that I understood this. I was reminded of the importance of the water and the time when I called to confirm my appointment. The FTS is also called a *nuchal fold screening*.

This space called the nuchal fold is an indicator for Down syndrome. According to Baby2see.com, which was an invaluable resource through my scans,

> The nuchal translucency is a collection of fluid beneath the fetal skin in the region of the fetal neck and this is present and seen in all fetuses in early pregnancy. The fluid collection is however increased in many fetuses with Down's syndrome and many other chromosomal abnormalities. It is called a 'translucency' because on ultrasound this appears as a black space beneath the fetal skin. (www.baby2see.com)

The translucency is measured using high-resolution ultrasound imaging. The space of the nuchal translucency fold and the presence of a nasal bone are soft indicators for Down syndrome. Fetuses with Down syndrome usually have a larger nuchal fold and no nasal bone.

The test measures other indicators of healthy gestation such as crown-rump length. Sometimes the results of the crown-rump length will cause your due date to change as it is a more accurate indicator of gestational age than the date of your last period. This test isn't just for gestational age and Down syndrome; there is an entire world of chromosomal abnormalities that can simply occur. Then there are all the genetic abnormalities that you and your partner throw into the pot.

Because my husband and I are both Italian, I was warned that my fetus needed to be tested for Mediterranean anemia, or thalassemia—which, according to the Mayo Clinic, is "an inherited blood disorder characterized by less hemoglobin and fewer red blood cells in your body than normal." Thalassemia is treatable; although inconvenient, it is possible to thrive outside the womb and have a decent quality of life, unlike the terrifying Tay-Sachs disease, which is a rare inherited disorder that causes progressive destruction of nerve cells in the brain and spinal cord. Although it is possible for babies born with Tay-Sachs to live outside the womb, quality of life is virtually nonexistent, and most babies will not survive the first five years of life. Of those five years, the majority will be spent hooked up to tubes in a hospital bed.

Then there are the Trisomy abnormalities—Trisomy 8, 9, 12, 13, 16, 18, 21, and 22. A Trisomy can occur with any chromosome, but often result in miscarriage. For example, Trisomy 16 is the most common Trisomy in humans, occurring in more than 1 percent of pregnancies. This condition, however, usually results in spontaneous miscarriage in the first trimester (http://en.wikipedia.org/wiki/Trisomy). Each chromosomal abnormality carries its own deformities and challenges, and in many cases, a fetus cannot thrive outside the womb.

Let's backtrack. Remember that part about me being skeptical and ridiculously informed? I'm not a medical doctor. I'm an educator. I know how to find credible sources, conduct research, analyze said research, and break it down into digestible pieces. That's my wheelhouse. Reading about chromosomal abnormalities for the first time was absolutely overwhelming. A simple Google search of "first trimester screening" can be a rabbit hole of terror and stress. I find this true anytime I google a medical condition. Oh, and when you have kids, that doesn't get any easier.

I had an OB appointment on December 30, where my doctor performed an ultrasound and took an image of the spinal cord. As soon as I made the appointment for the FTS, I began researching the first trimester screening and nuchal translucency scan. I also searched for images of normal and abnormal nuchal translucency folds. I wanted to know what the doctor and ultrasound technician would look for. Because I had done my research, I was not alarmed by the fact that she was meticulously checking out the spinal area of the fetus. She even gave me a picture of the fetus's spine.

6

Getting There Is Half the Battle

Jamie and I set our alarm clocks for 8:30 a.m. for a 10:20 a.m. appointment that is twenty minutes away from our house in Nutley, at St. Barnabas Medical Center in Livingston, New Jersey, which we will arrive at five minutes early (the way I like to). We went to sleep anxious and excited.

Around 7:00 a.m., we wake up to see snow falling outside, not picturesque flurries but heavy snow that is starting to stick. We scramble to get out of the house as quickly as possible.

That may seem easy, but we have three dogs that need to be walked. Plus there's a necessary trip to Starbucks for coffee. Oh, and I am battling some of the worst nausea I have ever experienced in my entire life by this point. So leaving the house in a timely fashion is a job unto itself. (I thought it was difficult before I had a baby, but that's another story.)

With the dogs walking, coffee in hand, we make our way to the highway bound for the hospital. Traffic on the Garden State Parkway is slow but moving. Remember, I have to drink twenty-five ounces of water thirty minutes before my test. What this really means is that I have to drink twenty-five ounces of water and hold it until my scan. On the parkway, heading for Route 280, it's 9:45 a.m. I begin my first sips of a thirty-ounce bottle of water as we drive across the overpass toward the merge onto 280. I see exactly what I was dreading. Traffic. Inclement-weather New Jersey traffic.

Put this on your "what if I'm ever driving through Essex County, New Jersey" list—if you can see the traffic backed up, don't get it. On Route 280, there is only one opportunity to avoid the traffic. You have to take the very first exit on the highway. It's one lane over from the on ramp, and it leads you through a very rough neighborhood.

Lucky for me, I grew up in this neighborhood. So I was happy to see the Central Ave, East Orange, exit. Jamie moves quickly, and before we know it, we are taking the back roads through East Orange all the way up to St. Barnabas Medical Center in Livingston.

I'm drinking and drinking, but when you are pregnant, you always have to pee. Now, it's 10:10 a.m., we're creeping through Essex county, and I'm still drinking and trying not to think about how much I already have to pee.

It's 10:14 a.m. and we have made it to the hospital parking lot. At 10:19 a.m. I signed into the office at the genetic counselor. We sit down, and I'm thinking, *We'll be called any minute. I'll be able to pee within the next half hour.*

In my rush to leave the house, I didn't bring anything to read and I forgot my phone.. My only option was to watch Wendy Williams. However, my ears soon wandered to the different discussions all over the room. Some women were there with their sisters, others brought husbands, and others brought their entire families. At this point, they all have one thing in common—they look like they have been there for a while.

You know how people who have been waiting for a while get the furrowed brow and scrunched face? You can see the tension in their bodies as they shift in their seats and check the time on their phones and watches. Each woman lets out a sigh of relief when her name gets called, they follow the genetic counselor into a room, and twenty minutes later, they return to the waiting area.

Some women returned to the waiting area with a prescription for more bloodwork, while others had charts and streamers of ultrasound pictures.

The woman directly across me sat beside her disinterested husband. She whispered tenderly to a series of ultrasound pictures while her husband played with his iPhone. He stopped what he was doing when the genetic counselor sat down with them to field any last-minute questions they may have about the Tay-Sachs test screening for which they had to make an appointment. I felt more like I was tuning into each conversation rather than blocking them out.

Now, it's 11:00 a.m. I have been waiting for forty-one minutes. Everything I look at reminds me of the fact that I have to pee—from Wendy Williams's thick, wavy hair flowing on her shoulders to the water cooler. I go to the desk and delicately say, "Excuse me, my appointment was for 10:20 a.m."

The receptionist curtly says, "We are seeing all patients today."

That was her way of telling me, "I really don't give a crap that you were here on time, lady, you're waiting, deal with it."

I leave reception and go directly to the bathroom. Screw these people, I'm peeing. I return to the waiting room and start drinking my water again.

I sit, I wait, I drink, and I watch. Some women returned to the waiting area with a prescription for more bloodwork while others had charts filled with stick people outlining how they are a carrier for some disease. All around me people were leaving with less than ideal news, characterized by tears or a wrinkly forehead but certainly not the smile of someone who has just seen their baby in high definition.

Finally, three hours later—that's right, at 1:30 p.m.—my name gets called. I am a little closer to getting out of this place. My technician asks me if I drank the required amount of water.

"Yes, I say, all 25 ounces."

"Twenty-five ounces, who told you that?" she asks.

"The receptionist who booked my appointment," I reply.

"Oh god, you only have to drink sixteen ounces. Your bladder may be too full," she says. (Understatement of the year.)

She leads us to a room with an examining table, an ultrasound machine, and a flat-screen monitor overhead. I fold down the top of my pants, and the technician takes a bottle of ultrasound goo from a bottle station. I'm thinking, *Wow, a warmer, I thought this stuff was famous for being too cold*, when the technician applies what has to be the hottest matter to ever touch my midsection.

For the first time, before we see the fetus, we hear its heartbeat. Then the technician runs the scanner over my abdomen. (By this time, the shock of the hot goo has worn off.) The fetus hates it, but the technician, who is grateful for our patience, takes lots of pictures. We watch the fetus on the overhead monitor while she scans and measures. I did my homework, and I have a good idea of what she's looking for, such as the presence of a nasal bone.

This creature was actually trying to dodge the scanner. The technician was chasing it around my abdomen.

"This kid is very stubborn, good luck to you," she says.

Ten years later . . . she was not fucking kidding.

7

Maternity Clothes

I decided not to buy any maternity clothes until after the first trimester screening. As a teacher, I eagerly awaited the opportunity to spend Christmas vacation in sweatpants. The universe had other plans. For the first time in my life, when all my pants—especially my jeans—are filled to capacity and I can't drink, every friend Jamie and I have asked us for double dates. None of our friends had kids yet.

You will find that this happens. A bunch of your friends will all get married within a few years of each other. Then you'll start having kids within a few years of each other. Someone always goes first, someone goes last, other people get divorced and go for the do over. In this particular situation, I was going first on the fetus train.

My sweatpants vacation was cut short when I needed an outfit for a dinner date with friends. My big maternity store trip was a few days away. (Of course I had this planned and the research completed too.) During a dog food run at Target, I quickly invested in a pair of maternity jeans and a black, V-neck maternity shirt. Although I didn't buy these things on sale, as I normally always wait for sales, these two items paid for themselves within weeks. Of all the maternity pants and jeans I would try on, none of them compared in comfort to my "Target jeans."

Even if you can get away with your prebaby clothes, you might find that you are expanding in sections of your body you didn't anticipate. Maternity clothes are designed to do the heavy lifting for these areas.

When I made my first voyage to a maternity clothing retailer, my husband came for moral support. It was my bright idea to go to the Motherhood Maternity Outlet; I wanted to stretch my maternity clothes budget as far as I could. The first mission was pants. We expected the walls of baby bellies and maternity bras, but the clientele was a bit more than I had planned on.

It was me and two other pregnant women. I brought my husband, and they brought *everyone* in their families—mothers, fathers, husbands, children, and brothers. The dressing rooms in maternity stores are very spacious. When your customers are already size challenged, it's nice to have a little more room to negotiate changing your clothes.

These ample dressing rooms were packed with these two women getting fashion advice from their families. In fact, it was so crowded, I was trapped. I was texting my husband from my fitting room to bring me a different size or style. It was even more frustrating that the employees at this store did nothing to weed some people out of the fitting room area. We left the store exhausted from fighting our way through the fitting rooms and with three pairs of pants.

Maternity clothes continue to evolve. They are easily accessible. However, if you are having trouble finding items that really work for you, visit a quality maternity clothing store. There's going to be more variety and helpful sales people. Learn from my mistake, skip the outlets. They are carried in almost every store. There are lots of choices online. I utilized a capsule approach to my maternity clothes.

If you want to look less pregnant, wear maternity clothes as soon as your clothes get tighter. Most likely, your pants will be the first thing to fill out. But one morning, you will wake up and your breasts will be one to two sizes bigger, so have a maternity bra ready to go. Forget about underwire. In fact, you should never wear underwear. You need to take care of your breasts, now more than ever.

Imagine a world of comfortable dress pants—the need to suck in your stomach is completely gone. All clothes are meant to make your midsection a more comfortable area. Imagine, no restrictive waistbands, no belts; shirts are a little longer, cut for a curvier you. I miss maternity clothes. I never thought I would be nostalgic for them, but they were the most comfortable clothes I have ever worn in public.

When I first planned on buying maternity clothes, I convinced myself that I didn't want to spend a lot on them because I would only be wearing them for a year. But after an honest look through my closet, I realized, who the hell am I kidding? Most of the stuff I buy at Kohl's is practically disposable clothing.

As a teacher, I can stretch a business casual wardrobe. The only time I have ever had to wear a suit is on job interviews. While I did decide to invest in maternity clothes, I did not want two wardrobes of maternity clothes. In other words, I didn't want work clothes and casual clothes. I wanted clothing that could multitask.

For the weekend, I still had my Target jeans. Foolishly, I thought I could do better with a pair of jeans from Motherhood, but here's the key to maternity jeans: you don't want heavy denim. When you are dealing with pants that have a nylon panel for a belly/waistband, heavy fabric will make them droop, despite your best efforts. My Target jeans were a lighter weight denim and stayed up. In fact, they did not look like maternity jeans at all.

At some point, you will have to decide what kind of pregnant woman you want to be. Do you want to embrace the belly or hide your belly? I'm not talking about exposing the belly—that is a different type of woman entirely—and if that's you, kudos. That's not my style.

If you want to embrace the belly, formfitting maternity knit shirts and T-shirts are very comfortable and easy to wear. In fact, the lack of bulk and excess material that is commonly used in empire waist maternity shirts can make you look less pregnant. However, an Empire waist (high waist, flowing shirts) that tie in the back can make you look much more pregnant. Nonpregnant women who wear empire waists look pregnant. It depends on your personal taste.

You may think that you won't need maternity shirts, but remember, they are cut to accommodate more curves. Not everything is Empire waists and baby doll shirts. I preferred the formfitting maternity shirts, especially short sleeve shirts and sweaters. Maternity T-shirts are ruched on each side to fit your belly without adding fabric everywhere else. Add a jean jacket, a cardigan or two, maybe a lightweight kimono or blazer, and you are in business. I also invested in a maternity store raincoat. It was a generously cut knee-length Empire waist trench. I was able to dress it up or down, layer underneath it, and it served well into postmaternity. In my wardrobe, I had capsule pieces such as the jeans, raincoat, and stretchy twill pants and T-shirts.

Aside from my Target jeans, my favorite pants were the Motherhood Maternity twill pants. These pants had buttons on the inside of the calf so that you can fold them up into a capri. I was due in July, so I wanted clothes that could go the distance.

Here's my list of recommended maternity wardrobe:

1. A nursing bra—the kind that holds the pads, one size up from what you normally wear.
2. A nursing tank top—to wear under your pajamas. Give gravity a hand. Keep the girls up.
3. Maternity tank tops—when you are pregnant, dressing in layers is key to keeping your nipples under control and controlling your body temperature too. (More on spontaneous sweating later.)
4. Two pairs of dress pants in neutral colors. I recommend black and grey.
5. A button-down shirt—the shirt, combined with dress pants, is good for more formal occasions. Very easy to dress this up with pretty flats and some jewelry.
6. Two sweaters that are long enough to cover your butt.
7. Maternity pajamas.
8. A pair of flats, half size bigger (or in wide). Don't buy these in advance.
9. A good pair of sneakers for the weekend. (Your back will thank you.)
10. Maternity yoga pants—sure, regular yoga pants in a size up could work, but maternity pants have softer waistbands and thicker fabric. You might have more area to cover.
11. Seven T-shirts.
12. Maternity underwear.
13. Postpartum compression belt—*not* a belly band.

These thirteen items may seem excessive, but you have bought more than this on a given shopping spree at least once in your lifetime. I'm not saying buy all this at once. In fact, if anyone you know offers you maternity clothes, take them! Yes, during pregnancy, there are many things you will need; and having a baby is expensive. Accepting gently used items from people you trust is an ecofriendly and an economical way to get what you need while sticking to a budget.

If you are among the first of your family and friends to embark on the baby journey, consider this guideline for shopping. On your first trip to the maternity store, buy jeans, two shirts, two pairs of pants, maybe a sweater/jacket, and a bra. Plan on going back twice in your second trimester and once in your third trimester. A multitude of T-shirts is important because, as you get bigger, you will be surprised at how much crap lands on your shirt. Your belly becomes a magnet for stains. I also suggest darker colors and patterns to camouflage any belly mishaps. I can't tell you how many times I rubbed my belly against the car and was dirty before I even got to work.

Also, as you progress in your pregnancy, you will begin to sweat like a teenage boy. I suggest switching to men's deodorant and wearing layers to hide the sudden "hot flashes." Obviously, you want to adjust some of these items based on when you are due. However, you will most likely buy the bulk of your maternity clothes in your second trimester. Don't buy anything too formfitting. If you are between sizes, go up a size to allow for the overall swelling that will take place in your third trimester.

Remember, you will wear maternity clothes for at least a month after you give birth. Maternity clothes are comfortable and stylish if you let them be comfortable and stylish. They are easy to wear and when you are caring for a newborn, you'll appreciate these clothes all over again. I wore my maternity clothes until they were literally falling off me. I wore my postpartum compression belt from the day after I gave birth until it no longer fit me, about three months postpartum. It was recommended to me by my chiropractor. It offers support for a wobbly midsection. It works for those who have vaginal delivery or C-section.

If you need to bind your breasts, you can even wrap it around your chest for relief. Your lower back will feel weak for months. Your body recovers from the delivery, only to begin the physical work of bending and reaching over for your baby. Hormones are still flooding your system, and you will need support. My favorite thing to do was to stick an ice pack in the back of my compression belt. It offered so much relief to a sore lower back. If I could only buy one item on my list, it would be number 13.

While many stores offer maternity clothes now, consider going to a maternity retailer at least once in your second trimester. Find what you like in store and replenish online. The same goes for a baby registry. These stores are trained to care for pregnant women. There are lots of places to sit and refreshments. The dressing rooms are spacious, and there are even baby clothes and nursing products.

8

Why Is It Called Morning Sickness?

By the sixteenth-week mark, I was in full baby swing. I updated my baby registry, I went to the doctor, and I did all this while riding a wave of nausea. People were still asking me how I felt, and whenever I told them that I was still nauseous, it was met with "Oh, that didn't stop for you yet?" No, it fucking hasn't. Unfortunately, I didn't vomit enough to keep weight gain at bay, but maybe I would have gained more than eight pounds in sixteen weeks, had I not been so sick.

At the doctor, I received a prescription for more bloodwork. Awesome! As if they didn't get enough from the last eight vials I've given over the past fifteen weeks.

Now let's talk about the headaches. From what I understand, they are due to increased hormone levels. (What else is new?) However, I get headaches when I drive, when I look at my phone, when I throw up, when I'm nauseous—so I pretty much get these headaches all the time. And all I can take is Tylenol. I might as well eat Pez.

By the end of the first trimester morning sickness wears off for most people. By week 16, it ramped up. Let me explain my journey. My pregnancy was confirmed at seven weeks. I had seven weeks of little to no nausea. I was, however, very thirsty. I remember never being able to drink enough water.

At week 8, I noticed odors. Well, everything seemed to turn into an odor. For example, after Thanksgiving, I was making turkey soup. I had a stockpot simmering on the stove. The aroma from this soup became so overwhelming, I kept moving to different rooms in my house to avoid it. Finally, convinced that this soup was too disgusting for anyone to eat, I threw it away.

All smells got me—peanut butter, soy sauce, the smell of lettuce, perfumes, soaps, and people, in general. Pregnancy hormones kicked my sense of smell into hyperdrive. Anything I smelled that didn't agree with me would send me into a cycle of dry heaving and vomiting. Couple that with motion sickness that showed up at the end of the first trimester.

While driving, I could actually make myself nauseated. I rode this wave of symptoms by adopting my doctor's motto, "The more symptoms the better." Everything was moving forward through a healthy trimester.

9

Baby Gear

The first time I tried to start my baby registry was a Saturday afternoon at Buy Buy Baby. I quickly learned that peak shopping hours are not the time for this.

I took my scanner and headed off to Baby Gear where my husband (who already has two kids) helped me separate the necessities from the crap. The entire way, we fought the crowds of "I am more important than you" pregnant women, their support teams, and the ability to monopolize an entire aisle. These instances make me think about the kind of pregnant woman I want to be. So far, I know the kind I don't want to be. Pregnancy is a time when you are getting reacquainted with your newish body. Personal space and social distance are always up for renegotiation. If you are sensitive to this, as I was, choose off-peak hours to shop.

When it comes to registering for baby gear, there are things that you need and things that you only think you need. My best recommendation is to work on your registry in pieces—don't try to do it all at one time. Consider having two registries, one at a baby store and one at a department store or Amazon. Start your in-person registry on a Saturday night or even a weeknight if you can. The store is more quiet, it's stocked and organized, and you have a shot at better customer service.

The purpose of the baby megastore is to make you believe that you need everything, especially when they package the baby-gear list in the handy registry welcome bags, which I like to call "baby swag." There's nothing like a free bib and window shade when you are about to embark on one of the most expensive ventures of your life.

10

The Baby Registry

One of the only things more daunting than being pregnant for the first time, with little to no baby experience, is creating a baby registry.

When Jamie and I got married, we completed a bridal registry. This was easy; we thought about the stuff we had and the things that could use an upgrade, and we registered. For example, dishes. Our chipped white setting for four gave way to Kate Spade for Lenox. We traded our IKEA silverware for Oneida. We received many generous gifts from our registry and continue to enjoy all of them, but we could have survived with anything or nothing. With a bridal registry, if you don't get something you registered for, chances are, you may not have really needed it. There's no one telling you that you must have this or that because an innocent life hangs in the balance of which bottle system you choose!

I entered the baby registry with the same "how much of this stuff do I really need?" approach, but that was before I realized that it's not for me. Ergo, the greater question became "How much of this stuff does the baby really need?"

Here's what it's like to register for baby gear. You fill out an application, complete with a due date, optional gender information, and nursery theme information. The only thing I knew was the due date. Then you get a gift bag with a parenting magazine and a few free gifts—a bib, a pacifier, a parenting magazine—I call this stuff "baby swag."

Here's the daunting part: No matter where you go, there will be some kind of folder, and therein is a list of *all* the things for your baby that *you* need. It is a tedious list. For example, the baby's health and grooming, the category may have three types of thermometers, baby Tylenol, teething gel, nail clippers, baby brush, baby comb, nasal aspirator (or booger sucker), diaper cream, shampoo, baby soap, lotion, nailbrush, massage lotion, bath music, bathtub, bath mat, bath toys, spigot cover for sink, all-natural sponge, baby shower gel, baby towels, baby washcloths, etc.

It gets to a point where you click away with the scanner or ask yourself, "How much will my baby really need right away?" and "What's wrong with the washcloths I already have?"

I tried to ask myself this very question with every category. I was lucky enough to have Jamie with me who has been through this, but a lot has changed in baby gear since his last child.

Granted, there were some things this folder told me that made sense. For example, don't just register for newborn items. Try to get things for the first year. Think bigger. Always go a size up. Kids will typically grow into clothes. (Side note: if your baby is a preemie, you won't use the newborn size for a while. If your baby is in the eight-to-ten-pound range, they will wear the newborn onesies for probably about a day.)

Registering for baby items took me three trips because I gave myself thirty minutes the first time and sixty minutes for the last two trips. Otherwise, it would have been too much. It's baby overload, and it's enough to make the sanest woman freak out.

The bottle aisle almost killed me. Jamie asked, "Have you decided on a bottle system?" I didn't even know what he meant. I have to commit to one style of bottle and stick to it? What if the baby doesn't like the one I choose? What if it has an allergy? Why does a bottle encompass an entire system? There were no answers.

I opted for the BPA-free bottles, chose some nipples, but I still have no idea what I was scanning. Evidently, the bottle system also includes bottle brushes, a spinning drying rack, a microwave sterilizing system, and assorted other items that I will have to find space for in my kitchen.

One area that I thought I would really enjoy would be selecting the crib and nursery colors, until I saw the prices. Why does a baby need a crib that will convert into a double bed with a sleigh headboard? What's the difference between a bassinet and a crib? What's a minicrib? Why is this changing table five hundred bucks? Can we go to IKEA now?

Your child does not need three thousand dollars' worth of furniture. You do not need a six-hundred-dollar glider. In fact, they will destroy this stuff like a rock star destroys a hotel room. Purchase what you need conservatively. If someone offers you something gently used and fairly new, strongly consider taking it.

It's been scientifically proven that patterns in black and white are visually stimulating to babies and increase their cognitive development. All I wanted was black and white. What you will find are neutral schemes. Grays, pastels—gender centric palettes. Don't fall for trends. Consider opting for science. Your infant can't read, so two hundred dollars in lettering to have their name on a wall is really more for you.

The registry experience made me realize that it's not about the stuff. Babies have been around forever—long before nasal aspirators, video monitors, and baby massage lotion. That's why we're all here. My best advice is don't let the baby megaretailers overwhelm you. It's intimidating but not impossible. Should an expectant parent skip an item on the registry? It's not as if the baby is going to pop out and say, "Hey, I specifically ordered the beige bassinet with the USB port!"

11

A Reflection on Baby Gear

Within the first two weeks of being home with your baby, you will quickly realize the things you need more of and the things that are taking up space. If I had to register all over again, I would do things a little differently.

There is a huge learning curve with baby gear. Your baby is not going to know that you selected a crappy bottle warmer or that he or she will outgrow the bassinet within the first three months. Oh, and the baby will definitely not know that a certain baby bible book told you to wash *all*—I repeat, *all*—the baby clothes to help with your nesting, even the clothes that the baby may outgrow before it is even born.

The good side is that I am very glad I did not know the gender of my baby when I selected my baby gear. Women only get one real chance to have a baby shower. While a second, third, or fourth child might bring a sprinkle or gentle upgrade of necessities, gender-neutral products allow you to plan for another child or give everything away if the "shop closes." This is also a great place to look to family and friends offering gently used donations. If you can avoid buying it and get it from a trusted source for less, do it.

It's good to register for items beyond the newborn requirements for a baby, but don't buy extra until after the baby is born. There are going to be things that your baby doesn't like. Also, avoid clothes that are made of polyester. Babies have very sensitive skin, and your baby may even have a skin allergy or eczema. You don't know yet. You can't go wrong with breathable all-natural cotton. Also, avoid scented bath products. Take the safe road and register for fragrance-free products.

Much in the way that there are parents who are quick to overprepare and purchase everything that they may ever need, as I was, there are also parents who are really afraid to overpurchase and take a minimalist approach to baby gear. I think that there needs to be a middle ground. If I had to do it all over again, this is the list of things I would buy:

1. Pack 'n Play with bassinet (that can be lowered) with a changing station.
2. Fisher Price bundle. (This is one seat that converts to a baby seat, baby swing, high chair, and toddler seat.)
3. Travel system that supports up to thirty pounds. For example, the Chicco KeyFit Travel System is a car seat, base, and stroller that supports your baby up to fifty pounds. If you get a car seat that only supports up to twenty to twenty-five pounds, you will have to replace it after the first seven months. Also, consider an umbrella stroller as a spare.
4. Skip the baby towels and invest in a few new cotton/terry bath sheets and washcloths. You will get much more use out of these.
5. Baby bath tub insert for your sink or tub that also holds a toddler—baby bath tubs are cute but kind of pointless. Fill a bucket and then dump the water all over the surface where you plan to bath the child. There. Now you have experienced what it's like to use a baby bathtub.
6. Toy box—you are going to have an abundance of toys, whether you want to or not. Be prepared by planning on an organized place to put them. (I am a firm believer in IKEA. IKEA offers an abundance of storage solutions, from hanging, multilevel mesh organizers [a good solution to a toy box because it does not have to go on the floor], to toy boxes, and children's furniture.)
7. A mini crib—don't bother with a crib that converts to a double bed; you may never use that.

8. All-cotton onesies, long sleeve with built-in mittens, sized 0–3 months. Your baby will grow into them within the first three weeks.
9. Baby nightgowns with built-in mittens—these are invaluable for changing a baby in the middle of the night. In fact, just keep your baby in these until he or she becomes mobile. If I was only able to buy one type of clothing for my baby for the first three months, it would be these.
10. Receiving blanket for snuggling and swaddling.
11. Breast pads—they stick to your bra. Think of them like panty liners for your boobs. Breastfeeding or not, if you have mammary glands, there's going to be leakage. Be prepared.
12. An Exersaucer—this gives babies a sense of independence. It keeps them interested and buys you some free time. The Evenflo Triple Fun Exersaucer converts into a play table and activity mat.
13. Diaper Genie with refills.
14. A Boppy (with an extra cover)—I don't recommend a Boppy for breastfeeding. However, for propping up your baby, for tummy time, and for when they are learning to sit up, a Boppy is a useful baby support pillow. It also aids in holding the baby.
15. My Brest Friend Pillow—I breastfed for all of seventy-two hours. However, I used my Brest Friend Pillow for the first five months after the baby. Holding and bottle-feeding a newborn puts a lot of strain on your neck and shoulders. This can affect your lower back too. It is just as important to support these areas of your body when you are bottle-feeding as when you are breastfeeding. This pillow wraps around your body and has back support. It also has a handy pocket to hold pacifiers or your cell phone!
16. Snuggle Nest—this is a folding, put-anywhere baby sleeper. It has two foam pillars to keep the baby from rolling. You can keep it in bed with you or put it in the baby's crib to keep them from rolling. It works for months. This saved me during the very early months, especially the first night home

from the hospital. If you want to keep the baby in bed for you, for any reason, it is the safest way.
17. Two packs of pacifiers—don't go crazy on the pacifiers because your baby may not like to use one or he or she may not like the type you selected.
18. Bottle system with sterilizer—even if you are breastfeeding, give your baby a bottle at least once a day. (If you are breastfeeding, buy or rent a breast pump.) Give your partner or the important people in your life a chance to feed and bond with the baby. Give yourself a chance to take a shower. Your baby is going to have to drink from a bottle eventually. There was no better feeling than handing a bottle and the baby to my husband and going to sleep. I love them both, but a girl's got to sleep.
19. Bibs and a package of cloth diapers to use as burp cloths—don't bother buying burp cloths; they are not big enough to control the drool and spit up.
20. A baby first aid/grooming kit—the American Red Cross makes a deluxe kit that has everything you need.
21. Baby monitor with camera and app for phone.
22. Happi Tummi—microwaveable baby heating pad. Also very helpful for sensitive tummies.
23. Groegg room thermometer.
24. Nightlight—this is more for you.
25. Diapers, wipes, and diaper cream for sensitive skin—Aquaphor is my favorite because it can be applied to any rashes or chapped areas, and it's good for cuticles.

As a woman who has also raised a toddler and a child. I highly recommend using a toddler bed when your baby begins to outgrow the crib. A toddler bed is inexpensive. They are closer to the ground, so they are safer than a "big kid" bed. It uses the crib mattress. They come in many different styles and with different characters. Let your child select their own bed. You will promote independent sleeping by getting him or her involved with their bed. Toddler beds use crib sheets and blankets so you can teach your child how to make their beds very easily.

Also, if your toddler has any bed-wetting or potty training issues, the crib mattress is easy to clean. Toddler beds can last until the baby is five or six years old. I attribute the size and accessibility of these beds to why my stepchildren have good bed habits today. They were able to learn how to make their beds. Also, they felt secure in a bed that was sized to them.

On another note, the law of twos—a great piece of advice I was given by many women was to have a changing area for every floor of my house where the baby is going to be. I also extend this to Diaper Genies. Ask yourself, *Am I going to run upstairs or downstairs every time I have to change or dispose of a diaper?* No, that's exhausting. Apply the law of twos.

If you only have one floor to your living space, consider just using a Pack 'n Play with a changing station instead of a crib. It's portable, and you will have more time to select the right kind of crib or toddler bed for your baby.

If you have more than one floor to your home, have a Pack 'n Play and Diaper Genie on the first floor of your living space. Keep another changing and sleeping area in your nursery or bedroom. Are you going to put the baby in the crib every time it falls asleep? Ask yourself this: Will your baby always be able to sleep in his or her crib when it's time to sleep? No. You will not always be home. Train your baby to be able to fall asleep anywhere. Leaving home will be much easier.

12

Breastfeeding

In breastfeeding, I pondered the wonderment of the five-hundred-calorie burn. I did just as I set out to—I tried to breastfeed. In the hospital, for the two nights and three days after I had Violet, I breastfed every two hours. I diligently had to report how long she fed on each breast.

And no matter what anyone else says—and not to be vulgar—it hurts like motherfucker. This pain is not only localized to just the nipple; it's nipple to shoulder. The baby latches or, worse, doesn't latch. If your baby doesn't latch, you have to keep trying to get her to latch on. Because if you don't, the pain is intensified and you have to feed longer. When people boast about the benefits of breastfeeding, they rarely address the issue of a baby's tongue. Not every baby has a tongue made for breastfeeding. If a baby has short frenulum, which can also mean "tongue tied," then he or she will have difficulty latching. Also, the size of a woman's nipples can impact the ability for a baby to successfully breastfeed. Your nipples may be Amazonian and choke the baby or they may be too small. Both issues affect latching. (Read this for more information: http://pediatrics.aappublications.org/cgi/content/full/110/5/e63.)

If you are modest like me, breastfeeding is also very isolating. Breastfeeding in front of people was not an option for me. Breastfeeding is often referred to as an on-demand process. This is because you don't track the number of ounces the baby ingests. You have to track how long you have fed the baby—twenty minutes on the right breast, twenty on the left, etc. Because breastfed babies have to work so hard to get the milk out, they will usually fall asleep while they are eating. Then you have to wake the baby, get him or her to latch, and repeat the process again.

When I first considered breastfeeding, I had never heard of growth spurts. Babies have these within the first few days after birth, every few days for weeks, and until about twelve weeks. During these spurts, they feed more intensely and sleep more.

For the first twenty-four hours at home, I breastfed. I was sleep deprived, uncomfortable, and stressed over caring for a newborn. But I kept going. By thirty-six hours, when the milk came in, my breasts became swollen beyond recognition (gross). This process is called *engorgement*. I remember sitting in bed, watching my husband sleep, and crying because I was so tired and no one could do this except for me.

That's when I said, "Screw this." In my kitchen were sample cans of formula. (Formula companies will send you full-size samples for free!) I handed a very cranky baby to her father, ran to the kitchen, and made a bottle. I gave the bottle to my husband, and I went to sleep. Violet finished her bottle and fell asleep, satisfied. I felt a little guilty. I comforted myself by thinking, *She was hungry and I gave her what she needed. Who cares if it didn't come from me?*

I pumped for a month. Eventually, you can't pump enough to mimic actual breastfeeding, and the milk supply diminishes. When you stop all milk stimulation, breasts will become engorged again, one last time. This is an extremely painful experience. You may want to pump to relieve some of the pressure, but that will only stimulate more milk. Your doctor can prescribe you medication that will help the milk dry up. Hot showers and cold compresses work well. I wrapped a postpartum compression belt around my chest, stuffed an ice pack in there, and took advice. Within eight hours, the engorgement subsided.

The bottom line is this: breastfeeding is an all-consuming process. Breastfeeding your baby does not make you supermom. Foregoing breastfeeding doesn't make you a slacker. Unless you have enough family support and help—I mean, around-the-clock help from a team of people to care for all other matters outside of feeding the baby—it's stressful. Don't believe the "breast milk is best" cliché. The best thing is for a baby to have a mother who isn't an emotional train wreck. At some point, you have to stop breastfeeding.

13

Whose Breasts Are These?

Like a travelling companion, breasts are always on a journey with you. In my emaciated late teens, I was a dainty 32A cup. By my early twenties—and thanks to being on the pill—I hormonally pushed myself up to B cup status. I was happy with a 34B cup. I went up to a C cup in my late twenties, after I started dating my current husband. I reached my limit at what I thought was an impressive 36C cup. Neither of these size increases were due to extreme weight gain, nor medical intervention.

I enjoy mobility. I mean, I like to move my arms without any obstructions. I enjoy sleeping on my side or stomach. I like that my bras are relatively attractive. They don't have the duffel-bag straps that old lady bras have. In fact, I have enjoyed moving up in breast size to look more like a grown-up.

I have been filling out my bras over the last five months. For example, in January, I bought two new sports bras—one was a medium (my size), and then I bought another one in a large because it was on clearance. That night, I tried on the large sports bra and started laughing at my reflection in the mirror. It was swimming on me. Six breasts could have fit in this thing. Four weeks later, I turned to the large sports bra in an attempt to avoid buying a new bra. I could not get it over *them*—the D cup sisters.

I have never seen breasts this big, and I have no idea how to contain them. I have to sleep on my side, despite the fact that one will crush the other in a fight for space. And no, I will not buy the Kush that looks like a dildo but is meant to separate the breasts of a pregnant woman—no, the Kush Support is just not for me.

Next, there is the cleavage to contend with. I have never had much cleavage before so I find this meeting of my breasts incredibly obscene. I can't do anything to hide it. I can't cross my arms because that makes it worse. Who am I kidding? I can barely cross my arms with these things in front of me.

In my own defense, I have not gained much weight over the last five months. In fact, I seem to be carrying most of the weight in my new enormous bra. My biggest fear is that they will continue to grow. And what about when I start breastfeeding? How do I not suffocate a baby with one of these? Furthermore, where do I go from a D? It's much too horrible of a thought. What have I gotten myself into?

Is the world staring at my breasts? Well, more of the world might be, once I publish this. My husband keeps pointing at me and saying, "Oh my god, that's awesome!" The running joke with him is that my breasts grew after we began dating. Now he believes he has a Jedi power that makes me go up a cup size every five years. I'm going to call these bags of hormones on my chest a side effect of pregnancy. But these "side effects" are warm, heavy, inconvenient, and uncomfortable.

Clearly another moment where the *What to Expect* bible failed me. Sure, they discussed the large breast issue. But no one ever talks about how these things feel or how to deal with them. No one has ever addressed the moment where I had to buy the large bra with the duffel-bag, old lady straps.

14

Breast Health

Seven years after the birth of my daughter, I underwent a prophylactic bilateral mastectomy with reconstruction after discovering that I had the genetic mutation BRCA2, which predisposes me to higher rates of breast and ovarian cancer. While this will be the subject of a completely new book, I learned something very important that needs to be shared here. According to my plastic surgeon, who deals exclusively with breast reconstruction, new mothers and nursing mothers must be extra diligent with monitoring breast health.

The mammogram of a nursing mother or of a woman who has recently nursed can look like a hot mess. They are very difficult to read because the ducts are filled with milk and residue. Also, women have a tendency to become so wrapped up in the care of their children that they neglect their own health. My advice? Don't do this. Continue to check your breasts regularly, before, during, and especially after your pregnancy. In fact, if you can get a clinical breast exam, mammogram, and/or MRI before you become pregnant, do it. Establish a baseline.

After you have the baby, stay on top of yearly gynecological visits. Don't stop getting checkups because you are not pregnant. Your life is important, and early detection is a lifesaving measure.

To that end, there are women and people who simply do not have the means to breastfeed. For example, if I no longer have mammary glands, if I were to have a baby now, I would not even be able to pump, let alone feed. At the end of the day, the most important nourishment is to feed your baby your way and use that time to be present—make skin-to-skin contact, make eye contact, and bond in a way that is meaningful to you.

15

A Reflection on Breasts

I was relieved when my breast size tapered off at a modest 38D. Have you ever seen a modest 38D? That's because there is no such thing.

You are pregnant—prepare for your body to take on a mind of its own. This will begin with your breasts. Regardless of how big or small you started with, by the end of the fifth month, you will look at yourself in the mirror in sheer disbelief of what you are seeing.

There is one thing you want on your side at this point—gravity. I don't care if you are one of the women who never wears a bra. Start. Just like you are on an emotional journey to motherhood, your breasts are on a journey too. You will be different at the end of this journey, and so will your breasts.

Just like with your stomach, your body can't expand that much and return to normal like nothing ever happened. Help gravity—don't fight it.

First, don't do what I did—don't continue buying bras in bigger sizes because your breasts are going to continue to change in size after you give birth. Invest in a few good maternity bras, now. It doesn't matter if you are going to breastfeed or not. Maternity bras are designed to (1) house those breast pads that I told you to buy in a previous chapter and (2) maternity bras keep the girls comfortable and supported.

I recommend buying two wireless soft maternity bras to sleep in. Yes, begin sleeping in these immediately. Gravity doesn't take a break, neither should breast support. For daytime, purchase two shaped maternity bras. These look more like regular bras. Go to a reputable maternity store. Remember, the majority of support in any bra is in the band, not the straps. Don't buy anything that only has one clasp. You are looking for at least two to three hooks for the daytime bras. The nighttime bras are like double-layer shelf bras that you slide over your head.

This is not the place to be frugal or a procrastinator. With maternity clothes, if you want to look less pregnant, wear maternity clothes as soon as your regular clothes get snug. (It's really no different with regular clothes. If your clothes are snug, go up one size and you look like you lost ten pounds.) It's the same with maternity bras. There is never anything attractive about muffin tops in your bras. You know when your boobs lop over the top of your bra so you look like you have four breasts instead of two? Never good.

You will wear these bras for months before and after you are pregnant, close to a year total. I know you have bought bras and worn them for a lot less time than that. I have a drawer full of bras, and I can tell you I don't wear all of them. Why? Because I didn't try on all of them in the store, and I didn't get help buying them from a professional. Don't make the same mistake. Your breasts will thank you, and with any luck, they won't droop down to your navel.

After you give birth, your breasts will leak. It is gross, I know. And for the nature women, earth mothers—it's a beautiful thing (if that's what you're into). I'm not.

I have had two encounters with lactating women that I will never forget. The first was during a hike around Walden Pond in Concord, Massachusetts, four years ago. My husband and I were enjoying an explorative walk around the pond on a beautiful August day in New England. The pond was filled with people playing the water and walking around the grounds. We were innocently walking past a family—a mother, father, and a toddler riding papoose style on her father's back. I glanced at the family as they walked toward me. This woman seemed to be sweating in a very peculiar pattern on her chest. Then I looked again. That wasn't sweat. There were two jangly breasts like milk pendulums swinging back and forth under a Grateful Dead T-shirt, spreading a layer of breast milk across the front of her shirt. She was totally unphased.

Jamie and I took one look at this as they were about ten feet away from us. Jamie said, "Please don't scream." He knew what we saw, and he knew I was being confronted with one of my worst nightmares—a lactating woman. I may have shuddered as she walked past. I cringed. It was too much woman and milk and crunchy granola-ness, even for Walden Pond. I figured this woman must be like a chupacabra, a passing sight that I would probably never see again.

That's until I went to the Bronx Zoo three years later. I'm innocently looking at monkeys when a pregnant woman with a baby in a stroller and the father walked past me. Again, no bra—tits swinging—this time, two vertical columns of milk streaking across her shirt.

The major lesson to be learned is, once your breasts are no longer totally flat, once there are mounds under your nipples, put on a bra. Keep it on. I have come to realize that it looks uncomfortable. It seems like two cruel sacks losing to gravity are pulling women down at the shoulders. If you're pregnant, make no mistake—you need a bra and breast pads. Wear them until you have completely stopped lactating. Please.

16

Cravings—It's Not Just Pickles and Ice Cream

At 8:55 a.m. one Friday morning, I sat at a computer during my teacher preparation period and had the following internal conversation with my fetus.

"You know what would be so good now? Red Sangria." a little voice inside my head said.

To which I replied, "Even if we could have Sangria, it's 8:55 a.m."

"It's five o'clock somewhere," said the little voice.

"No," I said.

Again, I wasn't actually talking aloud to myself. This was an internal dialogue between the fetus and I.

Everyone keeps asking me about cravings, but the only craving I get is for alcohol. I have wanted a margarita since December, and there was about a week in January when a cosmopolitan would have been delightful. This thing doesn't make me want the arbitrary, almost acceptable glass of red wine—it wants cocktails! The irony is that I have never been much of a drinker. With the exception of margaritas or a shot of José Cuervo Platino tequila, I keep my drinking to a minimum because I think I have the gene for alcoholism; but I don't know enough about my family history to know for sure.

Furthermore, when I was ten years old, I watched a movie of the week about a boy growing up with fetal alcohol syndrome. His sunken eyes and lack of fine motor skills scared the hell out of me.

Where there are cravings, there are also food aversions. Put ten pregnant women in a room together, and you will get ten different experiences of nausea. There is no rhyme or reason to what triggers sickness for different women. For me, it was smells and sights—the sight of raw chicken, the smell of onions, Chinese food, fish, roast turkey, soup. Also, temperature. I could not drink anything hot. My diet was relegated to iced coffee, bagels, yogurt, room-temperature pizza, cheese, Preggie Pop fruit-flavored lozenges (for morning sickness), and cupcakes.

Please note that there is not a chapter about this in *What to Expect*.

17

The Ultrasound and the Second Trimester Screening

There are three types of ultrasounds. There are the traditional ultrasounds that an obstetrician will perform in the doctor's office throughout a pregnancy to check for the basics—the presence of a gestational sac, a heartbeat, limbs and the general size of the fetus, and the amount of amniotic fluid. These ultrasounds look like satellite pictures. You have to know what you are looking at, and even then, most people end up just smiling and nodding at a seemingly abstract blob on a screen.

Then there are the high-resolution, 3D and 4D ultrasounds performed during the first and second trimester screenings by genetic counselors, perinatologists, and ultrasound technicians. The first trimester screening checks for the development of the spinal cord as an indicator of possible chromosomal defects and Down syndrome. You can hear the heartbeat and see the fetus swimming around on a flat-screen monitor above the ultrasound table.

The second trimester screening, or anatomy screening, checks for a plethora of things that could have gone wrong since the first trimester screening, including additional Down syndrome markers and spina bifida. This set of four blood tests and ultrasound screening is performed between the sixteenth and eighteenth week of pregnancy. AmericanPregnancy.com explains that the quad screen is a maternal blood screening test that is similar to the triple screen test (also known as AFP plus and the multiple marker screening).

However, the quad screen looks for not only the three specific substances evaluated in those tests (AFP, HCG, and Estriol) but also a fourth substance known as Inhibin-A.

The screen is essentially the same as the screening tests that look for only three substances, except the likelihood of identifying pregnancies at risk for Down syndrome is higher through the evaluation of inhibin A levels. The false positive rate of the test is also lower.

The lack of AFP levels is a possible indicator for spina bifida. The following is an explanation of the bloodwork and the ultrasound according to the Mayo Clinic:

> **Blood tests**
>
> The primary test used to check for myelomeningocele is the maternal serum alpha-fetoprotein (MSAFP) test. To perform this test, your doctor draws a blood sample and sends it to a laboratory, where it's tested for alpha-fetoprotein (AFP)—a protein that's produced by the fetus. It's normal for a small amount of AFP to cross the placenta and enter the mother's bloodstream, but abnormally high levels of AFP suggest that the fetus has a neural tube defect, most commonly spina bifida or anencephaly, a condition characterized by an underdeveloped brain and an incomplete skull.
>
> Some spina bifida cases don't produce a high level of AFP. On the other hand, when a high level of AFP is found, a neural tube defect is present only a small percentage of the time. Varying levels of AFP can be caused by other factors—including a miscalculation in fetal age or multiple fetuses—so your doctor may order a follow-up blood test for confirmation. If the results are still high, you'll need further evaluation, including an ultrasound examination.
>
> Your doctor may perform the MSAFP test with two or three other blood tests, which look for:
>
> - Human chorionic gonadotropin (HCG), a hormone produced in the placenta

- Inhibin A, another hormone produced in the placenta
- Estriol, an estrogen produced by both the fetus and the placenta

Depending on the number of tests, the combination is called a triple screen or quadruple screen (quad screen). These tests are commonly done with the MSAFP test, but their objective is to screen for trisomy 21 (Down syndrome), not neural tube defects.

Ultrasound

Many obstetricians rely on ultrasonography to screen for spina bifida. If blood tests indicate high AFP levels, your doctor will suggest an ultrasound exam to help determine why. The most common ultrasound exams bounce high-frequency sound waves off tissues in your body to form black-and-white images on a video monitor. The information these images provide can help establish whether there's more than one fetus and can help confirm gestational age — two factors that can affect AFP levels. An advanced ultrasound can also detect signs of spina bifida, such as an open spine or particular features in your baby's brain that indicate spina bifida.

In expert hands, ultrasound today is quite effective in detecting spina bifida and assessing its severity. Ultrasound is safe for both mother and baby.

Amniocentesis

If a blood test shows high levels of AFP in your blood but the ultrasound is normal, your doctor may offer amniocentesis. During amniocentesis, your doctor uses a needle to remove a sample of fluid from the amniotic sac that surrounds the fetus. An analysis indicates the level of AFP present in the amniotic fluid.

A small amount of AFP is normally found in amniotic fluid. However, when an open neural tube defect is present, the amniotic fluid contains an elevated amount of AFP because the skin surrounding the baby's spine is gone and AFP leaks into the amniotic sac. A second test can be done on the same sample to reliably confirm that a neural tube defect is present.

Discuss the risks of this test, including a slight risk of loss of the pregnancy, with your doctor.

I know all this seems a little unsettling, but it is your doctor's job to look for these things. The exciting part of this scan is that you have another opportunity to learn the gender of your baby. I was more nervous for the second trimester screening than I was for the first trimester screening.

The first trimester screening was private; it was just between the doctors, Jamie, and I. If something was wrong, no one would know, except us. It would be sad, but it wouldn't be public. I am not a very public person. It's ironic because I'm a writer—and one who specializes in creative nonfiction—but I will write about myself before I ever talk about myself.

Now, at eighteen weeks pregnant, everyone knew I was pregnant. If something was wrong now, it would be more difficult to deal with because it would be a more public issue. I remember thinking that had I known there would be another chance for things to develop improperly with the fetus, I would have waited until after the second trimester screening to make the news public.

Here's how mine went.

Jamie and I make it to the perinatologists, the same place we went to for the first trimester screening, excited but with the fearful trepidation that we will be stuck at this office for at least five hours like the last time. Luckily, we are called immediately for our appointment. This time, I didn't have to drink my weight in water, so that immediately made this experience better.

The technician shows Jamie to the ultrasound room and then pulls me aside. She says, "This is routine, but I have to ask, is it okay for the doctor to speak freely in front of your husband?" I answer *yes*, but in the back of my mind, I can't help but wonder what had to happen to make that question part of the basic procedure.

I learned along the way that this is for people in abusive relationships. It gives them an opportunity to ask for help. I just feel like more places should do this when couples go to appointments together.

Jamie is seated in a corner next to the table where I lay at a forty-degree angle. Scalding-hot ultrasound jelly is applied to my abdomen and smeared around with the ultrasound scanner. First, the technician checks the heartbeat. The screen monitor is filled with a blurry black-and-white image that looks like craters on the moon. Then she switches to 3D, and these craters become a twelve-ounce fetus wiggling around and shielding his or her face from the camera. The technician says, "The first series of scans are routine. They may not look like much, but we are checking the anatomy of major organs and soft indicators for Down's."

Okay, here it goes:

- Heart—four chambers pumping.
- Kidneys—two in full working order.
- Brain—fully developed.
- Palette—no cleft.
- Middle joint of pinky finger (Down's soft indicator)—visible. Ten fingers.
- Fully developed feet.
- Finally, genitalia are intact.

Then the technician tries to give us a view of the face. We see the eye sockets and ears, but my kid, staying consistent, turns around and keeps its back to us the rest of the time. No matter which way the tech makes me turn, no matter how hard she jabs that scanner into my stomach, it hides its face. Then it does one more trick for the camera, one "farewell until July" gesture—it raises its little fist and one finger.

Our baby flipped us off.

The room became quiet. Jamie, the technician, and I stared at the screen. The technician was quick to take a picture of the moment, saying, "You don't see that every day."

We were prepared for thumb-sucking and some other cute shenanigans, but "the finger"?

We left the doctor's office with a small stack of pictures. We walked past the other expectant mothers and fathers, intently studying their own ultrasound pictures, whispering, "Oh, how cute." It was a very defining moment. I think it indicates that a sense of humor may be genetic and this should be one hysterical kid.

18

Kids, Not Clones

In my family it was not uncommon for a pregnancy to be more of the engagement ring of the relationship. In some instances, it could be considered the test that the man had to take. Pregnancy could also be the glue that you hope will hold a cracking relationship together. While this is possible, the glue may not hold for very long.

The most disturbing reason I have heard in my family for why people have babies (and I don't limit this reason to my family alone) is "I want someone to love me." This argument assumes that the future person will love you unconditionally regardless of the horrible situation you may be bringing it into. This argument resonates with me because when I was a child, I heard a family member say it while she was eighteen, pregnant, and totally unprepared. It's no surprise that she turned out to be a terrible mother, always choosing herself and her own happiness over the needs of her children.

I understand the floor can drop out at any moment. I'm sure when my mother had me, she was not hoping that her marriage would end and she would be raising me with her parents. I'm pretty sure that my mother did not aspire to move back home with her parents, only to end up supporting everyone there. These experiences taught me a valuable lesson at a very young age: do not even think about having a kid until you are absolutely secure. This does not mean marry or marry well. This means that I needed to have the skills, independence, and self-preservation of a superhero. That's what I did. I mastered the ability to support myself and others. It's a fiercely independent survival skill with no safety net. That was the first step.

The second step was to decide if I really wanted kids and why. For me it came down to wanting to share my experiences with someone and to see what kind of contribution I could create for the world. But this did not come until I met my second husband. In fact, with my first husband, I was dead set against having kids because he struggled to maintain gainful employment and wanted me to support him while he lived comfortably in the extended dysfunctional womb of his mother's basement. While he was fun in a low-key sense in my early twenties, by my late twenties (after I made the mistake of marrying him), I had emotionally outgrown him many times over.

The third step was to realize that I am not creating a mini me. I am not creating someone who is under any requirements to love me unconditionally. I am responsible for giving this person everything I possibly can and then some. My job doesn't end when I think it's as good as I am. No, this person will need the tools to be better than me. That's what I hope.

Although my mom shared this philosophy with me, she was the one who made me stay in college and be able to support myself. Sometimes I feel like she is testing me. If we don't like the same things or share the same opinion, then I think she gets a little upset. I don't think she is alone here. What I notice with some parents is the desire to have a clone instead of a child. I do not want a mini me. I want to share in my child's interests, especially when they are different from my own.

If I knew that my kid would be just like me, then I would not have kids. Who needs my neurosis and pessimism? Who needs my hypochondria and anxiety? My job as a parent is to make sure that this person evolves into who they want to be and not the mirror images I may impose onto it. Sure, I have some qualities that I think would benefit someone else. If my kid is the next leader of the Republican Party, at least the choice will be their own. I will keep my mouth shut, wish them the best, and cry myself to sleep.

Finally, my kid couldn't have been more planned. It was because I wanted to make sure that my security level was at the highest I could get it. After generations of the women in my family having babies and having the kid's crib in their childhood bedroom, I hope that my pattern is a step toward a much more positive tradition.

19

Baby Nightmares: Quick, Before I forget!

Lately, my mind is a sieve. Normally, I have an excellent long-term memory. My short-term memory works very quickly, and I typically rely on lists so I don't overlook anything important. When I first got pregnant, I read about memory loss or "baby brain." This was an understatement.

Today, not only do I forget little things—like what day it is or what appointments I have—but I also forget larger-scale items like finishing painting the basement. Last night, I was in my basement doing laundry. I took a good look around and thought, *This place is in shambles.* Then I saw the can of paint and roller in the corner from three weeks ago. I thought, *Damn it! I forgot to finish painting!*

I forget time, what month it is. I forgot to change the calendar. In my house, it's still January. I forget where I put everything. I spend most of my day looking for things. I have forgotten words, what they mean, and how to spell them. In my line of work, that's a problem. So before I forget to discuss this next topic, there is one thing that has managed to make its way into my long-term memory—nightmares.

The most popular baby book in the land says that it is perfectly normal to have strange dreams about being pregnant while you are expecting. I was ready for a few cute dreams about babies, maybe bringing it home or what it would look like. If you go to www.thebump.com or www.babycenter.com, there are many discussion boards where you can share your strange dream stories. Enter these forums with caution and stay away from the dark side.

I usually remember about one baby nightmare a week. Obviously, there could be more. Two stand out to me. In the first dream, I am home with the baby. It appears to be my first day home from the hospital. I am alone with it, and I think my husband is at work. The day is going along fine. It's warm and sunny, and the child is agreeable, sleeping and eating. It rarely cries. Then Jamie comes home and tells me the house smells like urine. That is when I realize that I have forgotten to change the baby's diaper all day. I am filled with shame and embarrassment as Jamie proceeds to clean up the baby and make up for my negligence and insane lack of mothering.

In the second dream, I am in labor. The hospital looks like a country-style bed-and-breakfast. The room smells like mold. There is a priest sitting at the foot of my bed, and he's watching a black-and-white television. My dead grandfather is watching TV with him. Jamie's looking out the window. I'm sedated, and my arms are restrained to the bed. (In real life, I am not religious and I hate B and Bs.) My glasses have been removed so I can barely see. I know I'm in labor because I'm in pain, but everyone keeps ignoring me and saying it's not time yet. The vibe reminds me of the last scene in *Rosemary's Baby* but without the Japanese man taking pictures. That one really freaked me out.

Fortunately, I'm not alone in the baby dream department because my husband and my mother are having them too. Jamie said he had a dream where I was in labor and no one was telling him what was going on and he missed the birth.

In my mother's dreams, she's at her grandmother's house and everyone is staring at the baby as it sleeps in the bassinet in the kitchen. The logical side of me says that clearly the dreams are subconscious manifestations as the brain cleans itself out every night.

I'm glad I'm not alone with the dreams, but if there is one thing I wish I could not remember, it would definitely be these.

20

Pre Baby Preparation

A part of the baby process I never considered in the beginning was the level of home maintenance that would commence once there was actually a baby on the way. Foolishly I thought that buying a house and getting settled would be the most difficult part of the pre baby journey. I do not shy away from home repair and maintenance—in fact, I really enjoy it. Preparing to have a baby can change the way anyone looks at their home.

My house is clean and the clutter is curbed. My house is old and requires some extra TLC as a result of its age, but when I look around the house at the light sockets and wires, a few areas of chipped paint, and the cobwebs—that's when I think, *Is this place a death trap?* That's when I have to talk myself in from the ledge. That's when I write a list of the prebaby preparations.

The list is extensive but not insurmountable. In fact, it's a logical list of things we have wanted to do but put off for a while. For example, reorganizing the basement to include a kid-friendly TV area, changing the blinds to shades and repainting the living room, and not to mention buying a new couch that can stay dog-hair free.

The logical side of me says, "Slow down, what's the rush of babyproofing? This kid isn't going to be able to move independently for months!" Then I think, what if I don't have the time to buy them?

Nesting is a common instinct when a baby is on the way. It's different for everyone. It can manifest by the desire to scrub every square inch of your home with a toothbrush. It's decluttering, cleaning, organizing, and babyproofing on steroids. I think of it as "nesting anxiety." It's a sudden misfire in the brain telling you to take action. The nesting itself is relieved by the action. Cleaning and organizing can reduce anxiety. It gives you control during a time when everything seems uncertain.

The skeptical side of me (me, skeptical, *really?*) believes that this babyproofing stuff is hype. I grew up in a household that did not believe in babyproofing, monitoring television, or nutritional needs. My family raised children using two fundamental rules: don't lose the kid and don't let it die. It's not babyproofing; it's character building—survival of the fittest. Imagine if the Addams Family opened a nursery.

My mother likes to reminisce about how she let my grandfather babysit me, one night, when I was nine months old. She came home to find me awake, sitting on the kitchen floor in a diaper that was sealed with duct tape. I am perfectly safe and happy, playing with an empty wine bottle.

In the back of my mind, I am always shutting out the image of the wine-bottle-wielding, duct-tape-diapered baby girl; but in the end, it made me, *me*. So my biggest question is, Can all the babyproofing and monitoring, overprotective child-rearing inhibit a baby's ability to thrive creatively?

21

A Reflection on Pre Baby Preparation

Nesting is a real thing and it will exhaust you. However, everyone nests differently. Some women cook tons of meals; others obsess about the nursery. I repainted two rooms in my house and bought new furniture. I also cooked double for a while and froze a few meals. I made sure my freezer was stocked with easy go-to food choices that were fast to cook.

It's not until the baby is born and you carry it around the house that you realize how much babyproofing needs to be done. I remember thinking, *Were there always this many sharp edges in this house? When did the floor get so squeaky?* Every observation you make is heightened.

Nesting will continue when you come home from the hospital. Be as prepared as possible for your new arrival. I recommend three central tips for preparing your house for a baby:

1. I suggest taking the advice of the late Tracey Hogg, also known as "the Baby Whisperer"—take the seals off any bottles you may need. Sterilize some bottles and stock your diapers and wipes.
2. Declutter—this will make it easier to clean. Empty a cabinet in your kitchen for bottles, formula, pacifiers, etc.
3. Reserve a space on your kitchen counter for making bottles and sterilizing baby items.
4. Make a space in your bedroom or nursery for putting the baby to sleep and feeding. You want a comfortable area away from stimuli.

5. Decide if you are going to have baby items in every room of your house or if you are going to contain the baby-ness to a single room. I have a little bit of baby stuff in almost every room.

I knew I would be working from home so I put a baby swing next to my desk. I have the pack and play (with changing stations in my family room. I also planned on this area becoming the central play area for the baby because it is close to my work area and the kitchen.

I keep the high chair in the dining room and I have a baby seat (that attaches to the counter or table top) in the kitchen. At first the baby will be a little blob, so you will need to keep it in a baby seat that will support its head. Every month your baby will develop and make life a little easier for you. Once they can sit up on their own, you will be able to eliminate some baby seats and few baby items.

I don't mind having baby items around my house, so long as there is a reserved place for this stuff in every room. If I can contain it, that's okay. This time in your child's life seems like an eternity, but it goes by very quickly. Before you know it, he or she will be playing independently in their bedroom and you will wonder what happened to all the little baby things. Enjoy the baby-ness. Embrace it.

22

Prenatal Pampering and Self-Care

During my second trimester, I experienced my first professional massage. My dear husband, who may spoil me more than necessary while not excessively, treated me to a prenatal massage and facial.

I have had a professional facial in the past, but my central quirk is that I don't like strangers touching me. I don't mean doctors or medical professionals; I'm not that far gone. However, the idea of a masseuse took me a while to get accustomed to. I liken it to the first time I had a pedicure. I thought the prospect of someone tending to my feet was a strange concept, now I don't really mind it. However, I have gone to the same nail salon for three years.

I have had the same hair stylist for four years because I like to think that I avoid excess (like tanning) and stick to mainstream grooming—hair, nails, skin care, and associated products for maintenance. Being pregnant throws a wrench into vanity. I appreciate the compliments that "I'm glowing," although I just think I'm excessively puffy. My skin is luckily still decent, my nails have never looked better, but my hair is growing at Rapunzel-like speed.

Consider beginning a meditation or grounding practice. Sit quietly with your feet on the ground, rest or close your eyes, and breathe in for a count of four and exhale for a count of four. There are many meditation apps for grounding practices but starting simply, without the aid of a device, will give you a tool to help you during the stressful days to come. Babies can feel your energy. If you are stressed they can tap into that. Try the breath count technique while you have time to figure out what will help you rest and reset.

So what's my problem with the massage? The idea of someone rubbing my body rubs me the wrong way. When Jamie first surprised me with the gift, I was a little nervous. Have I mentioned that I am terrible with surprises? I'm not ungrateful, but my inner Vulcan prevents me from showing too much emotion. In fact, I am nervous but excited for the experience of forcing myself to have excess pampering.

At the Edamame Prenatal Spa, I had a personal spa day. The facilities are intentionally small to allow for a very intimate setting. The spa consisted of about six rooms. There was a room with locked closets for my belongings, a massage room, a facial room, a restroom, and even a shower. Every space was decorated in earth tones with light fabrics. There was soothing music and a water feature. It was very relaxing.

I realized that part of my hesitation might be having to be around someone else who was also having a spa day. I likened it to a nail salon. Sometimes the woman next to you is annoying or talks very loudly on her cell phone. Here, it was just my masseuse, Blair and I. She was very friendly, gave me a skin consultation, and survey before we began; and then she talked me through every step of the process.

First, I had a thirty-minute facial with a neck massage and eye treatment. Afterward, I had a fifty-minute prenatal massage. It was one of the most pleasant experiences I have ever had. Not once did I feel awkward or uncomfortable. In fact, I plan on booking something for my third trimester. I wonder if women fake pregnancy just to go back to this spa? Hmmm. I must admit I love it when my inner skeptic is proven wrong.

I can't stress self-care during pregnancy. This baby will arrive, for better or worse. You will be thrown into an overwhelming abyss of a life being dependent on you. Get the massage. Get the haircut. Don't hesitate. Look at it as nesting for your body.

23

Taking Time for Yourself

Now that you are pregnant, your personal time is at a new premium. Your body is changing, and soon your entire life and schedule will be too.

Physically, as soon as you get pregnant, start stocking up Palmer's Cocoa Butter body lotion for stretch marks. Your skin is about to go through a lot. Apply this lotion to your tummy, breasts—anywhere that runs the risk of stretching. You can't overmoisturize at this point. Also, moisturize from the inside out by drinking plenty of water and cutting back on salt.

Baths aren't always recommended when you are pregnant. Start getting manicures and pedicures. This is budget-friendly pampering that gives you some time off your feet, which some of you may not be able to reach for much longer. Once the baby comes, you may not have time to get your nails done. Also, you will be using your hands so much that it may not even be worth it. Resist the urge to nest by taking at least 30 minutes to sit down and rest every day.

24

Freakish Body Changes

As your belly starts to grow one of the first things you may notice the line that is darkening and spreading up and down the center of your body. It's called the *linea nigra*. This line develops as the muscles in your stomach begin to spread and separate. It's different for everyone. For some people, it is very dark and wide; on others, it's a skinny line.

You will have this line for months before and after you give birth. Parenting Weekly says,

> You have probably never noticed the pale line, called the linea alba, that runs from your belly button to the top of your pubic bone. It is usually the same color as your skin, but during pregnancy this line may darken (usually during your second trimester) and is then called a linea nigra (Latin for "black line"). This darkening is caused by increases in estrogen and progesterone, which in turn step up production of the pigment melanin, a condition known as hyperpigmentation. There is nothing you can do about it. It's best to just leave it alone.

I didn't find the linea nigra quite as unsettling as the spreading of my belly button. I was not one of those women whose belly button popped out or unraveled. I have a hypothesis that this only happens to very skinny women. I had a little extra, umm, "room" around my midsection when I got pregnant, and so I think my body didn't have to stretch quite so much as other women. *What to Expect* tells you to embrace the belly button. I was freaked out by it, but there is nothing you can do about it. Some websites suggest that you can cover it up with a band aid. I recommend wearing layers if you are concerned about it protruding. If your central concern is a belly button piercing, take it out.

Carpal Tunnel Syndrome

By far, the worst freakish pregnancy ailment that I experienced was carpal tunnel syndrome. Pregnancy Today explains that carpal tunnel during pregnancy is a byproduct of pregnancy:

> Excessive skin under the chin, fat ankles and chubby cheeks aren't the only byproducts of water retention during pregnancy. Extra fluid can also lead to repetitive strain illnesses (RSIs), a group of ailments that can be an annoying—if not disabling—nuisance for expectant moms. Carpal tunnel syndrome (CTS) is a painful problem that 28 percent of pregnant women have to endure.

The bones in my wrists were protruding so severely that I thought I dislocated something. I had weekly chiropractic treatments to adjust the tendons. Unfortunately, I had carpal tunnel and extreme numbness and tingling that lasted for approximately four months after my daughter was born.

This isn't just uncomfortable and inconvenient. It was frustrating before I gave birth. After I gave birth it was an impossible ailment. I had constant numbness and tingling in my fingers. My wrists ached, I couldn't grasp anything, and I kept dropping things.

Trying to open a baby bottle or even grab a bottle while holding the baby felt like an impossible task. Mornings were especially difficult because my wrists hurt and the numbness was worse. It took months for it to go away. It seemed to peak the first month after I gave birth, but it subsided and was gone within five months. Hormones—haven't they done enough?

Relaxin

It's a funny name right? Well, it's also the hormone that majorly invades your body when you are pregnant. According to MedTerms, *relaxin* is "a hormone produced during pregnancy that facilitates the birth process by causing a softening and lengthening of the cervix and the pubic symphysis (the place where the pubic bones come together). Relaxin also inhibits contractions of the uterus and may play a role in timing of delivery. Relaxin works by simultaneously cutting collagen production and increasing collagen breakdown."

The problem is that while relaxin sets out to do its job for your pelvic bones, all your joints also become more flexible. That's not completely good. Most back pain is in pregnancy, and it contributes to ailments like carpal tunnel syndrome. After you have given birth, this is where that postpartum compression band will become your new best friend. It will provide support when you're riding waves of relaxin. It will reduce the possibility of throwing out your back.

Of all the freakish changes in your body that you may experience, the one that rocked me more than anything was the emotional change. You don't need to be an expert researcher; you just need to be full of hormones to understand how these things take over your body and change how you process emotions. It's not like I became a pod person or anything, but I am not much of a crier. Also, I handle stress fairly well. I have a high tolerance for it.

One week before I found out I was pregnant, I had the parent-teacher conference from hell. For the first time in my career, I had a mother, who was also a colleague, yell at me as she defended her overcoddled, slacker son. I wanted to talk to her about his progress and behavior, and she wanted to scream at me and intimidate me.

I went home that afternoon and actually cried. I never cry. But this day, I cried because I hated my job, I hated this kid, I hated his Kate Gosselin–haired mother. I hated the fact that I was crying.

A week later, with my life back into focus, I found out I was pregnant. My first thought was, *Oh, that's why I cried last week.* I actually felt relieved that there was a medical, tangible reason why I couldn't handle a stressful situation.

Over the course of my pregnancy, I noticed that stress set me off faster than before. Once I was worked up, I could feel the blood rush to my face and could feel myself getting upset. My pulse would race, my ears get warm, and, despite my best efforts, it was difficult to calm down. My ultimate goal was to avoid stress. That's like trying to avoid air.

Then the crying started. Prebaby me was half Vulcan. I get pregnant, and suddenly I am completely human. Commercials made me cry. Baby clothes made me cry. A messy bathroom made me cry. The tears don't stop, but I am glad they have tapered off for a while.

Years later, there is a stronger emphasis on mindfulness, presence, and mediation. Years after giving birth, I became a certified yoga and meditation teacher. Learning the practice of meditation has completely changed how I processed stress. I wish I had the tool then that I have now to manage my emotions. I learned very late that I don't have to hide my feelings, and that's now how to manage anything.

A common question I get is, "What kind of meditation do you prefer?" I really like the kind where I sit still and breathe. That's all it is—finding stillness and noticing my breath. This will help you with all phases of conception, pregnancy, and parenting.

25

Support

A few years ago, a handful of teachers in the school where I worked were all married within about a year of each other. Now, that same handful are all pregnant and due within months, even weeks, of each other.

If there is anything this book shows, it's the range of emotions, concerns, and skepticism that pregnancy has brought with it. There may be tons of books and websites to read, but few things are more helpful than having other women around in the same situation. It's continual moral support. There is a comfort in knowing that you are not the only person who is completely winded after climbing a flight of stairs to use the bathroom for the tenth time.

The entire process of pregnancy from trying to conceive to after the birth is overwhelming. I understand why so many women experience extreme anxiety, stress, and even depression with this experience. The flip side is that it is also a very exciting time, and there is much to talk about and plan for. It is even better when you have people to go to, in addition to your family.

Here are six tips for a sane pregnancy:

1. Find a group of women to rely on for support.
2. Utilize social networking sites for support if you feel like there is no one around to whom you can relate, which is why I am writing this book.
3. Stay away from baby chat rooms—there is a dark side to pregnancy, and chat rooms are the portal.

Let me take a sidebar here. In my search for online mommy support and the perfect prenatal website (of which there are none), I used www.babycenter.com to look at chat rooms for women who were due in the same month. I found the July 2010 chat room. I was scrolling through the posts when I noticed that some women had also listed their other children. For example, some women have lists, similar to the following, under their signatures: mom to baby girl, baby boy, and angel baby girl. Angel baby? What's an angel baby?

I keep scrolling through the posts to find another woman with an "angel baby" that is hot-linked. Before accessing the link, I read the responses to whatever she had posted, and there were many. All these women were thanking her for sharing her beautiful angel baby with them. I had a sinking feeling that whatever I was about to click on could not be good. I clicked anyway and was brought to www.missingangel.org where parents can post portraits of their stillborn babies. Apparently, there is an entire industry dedicated to portraits of dead babies.

I understand that the only thing worse than a miscarriage is a stillbirth. According to SharedJourney.com, the difference is that "a stillbirth is the loss of a fetus after the 20th week of development, while a miscarriage refers to a loss before the 20th week." Either way, these are devastating experiences. The later on in the pregnancy, the worst it must be. So many women experience multiple losses on the journey to have a healthy baby.

However, I strongly urge pregnant women to avoid these websites. Don't go there until it happens to you. The images of dead babies are literally burned into my consciousness. Let's face it, these websites represent healing from some of the worst-case scenarios. I truly admire the strength of parents who have suffered such terrible losses. Expectant parents—I am telling you to avoid these websites, not from a place of insensitivity. Pregnancy is scary and stressful enough. When your baby is born, you will have plenty of time to worry about accidents.

Many of these websites are about parents trying to heal and move on. However, not every parent who suffers a stillborn birth is capable of moving on. This is the darkest side of all. It is an indescribable level of mourning. I liken these websites to headstones at a cemetery. Both are chilling. The bottom line is this: If this is your first pregnancy, you are already scared half to death. Every day is a journey of symptoms you have never felt before and little things to scare you. These mini mysteries build, and they are not solved when the day is done. Don't deliberately fuel the stress fire by going in search of worst case scenarios.

Back to the list, Clearly, pregnancy can take your mind and body to places that will scare the shit out of you. Pardon the vulgarity, but seriously back to the list.

> 4. Find a parenting class or exercise class in your area to meet other mothers. Unfortunately, most yoga classes are only mommy and me. What's even worse is that they have a tendency to cater to stay-at-home moms. It's nearly impossible to find a class in the evening. So consider leaving the baby with your partner one night a week or during the weekend and taking a class to get out of the house. Consider joining a book club. Those are free, and you can always listen to books on tape. Do not attempt prenatal yoga on your own, unless you have an already established yoga practice.
> 5. Find a class or group to visit after the baby is born. Many hospitals offer new mom groups. While these are helpful, sometimes they are not always convenient. My hospital offered a group that was at 9:00 a.m. on Monday mornings. That's an impossible time if you have been up half the night with a newborn or if you work.
> 6. Write about how you feel or find another creative outlet. If you have a group of friends in the same situation as yourself, set up a monthly meeting or "parent playdate." Whatever you do, acknowledge that support will help keep you sane. Don't isolate yourself. This is a life experience where it is more important than ever to interact with others and form new relationships. There are other people who feel the same way you do. You are definitely not alone.
> 7. You could take a prebaby parenting class. If neither you nor your husband have absolutely no experience with a baby, I

highly recommend it. Your ob-gyn can usually recommend a class in your area. They are typically run by your hospital.

8. Read a book about babies. At some point, you are going to ask yourself, *What do I do with it?* Prepare yourself a little. A friend of mine suggested I read *The Baby Whisperer Solves Your Problems* by the late Tracey Hogg. This book saved my life. Even now, I use it as a reference whenever I need advice. Hogg teaches you how to get your baby on a routine—a simple order of operations, not a schedule. She talks to you about how to prepare for the baby's homecoming. I wish I had this book before I was pregnant. I read it when my daughter was three weeks old. It instantly helped me. Hogg relies on the EASY method—"Eat, Activity, Sleep, Your Time." This simple order helps you predict your baby's needs and gives you some downtime in the process. It's supported at your fingertips. You may plan on winging it. Some people say that you can't get a baby on a schedule. I don't believe any of it. What I have learned is that children thrive on structure, especially babies.

26

The Glucose Tolerance Test

The glucose tolerance test has become a rite of passage for pregnant women at the end of their second trimester. It comes at a lovely time when your chest cavity is full of babies. There is literally someone laying on your chest and giving you the superpower to burp like a frat boy.

According to WebMD, the glucose tolerance test or (or GTT) is "the oral glucose tolerance test (OGTT) measures the body's ability to use a type of sugar, called glucose, that is the body's main source of energy. An OGTT can be used to diagnose prediabetes and diabetes. An OGTT is most commonly done to check for diabetes that occurs with pregnancy (gestational diabetes).

This test determines if you have gestational diabetes. Gestational diabetes can cause high birth weights in babies, among other mother-related health issues, but I'm not here to freak you out. Your ob-gyn will write you a prescription for bloodwork, but it's not that easy. At this point, every pregnant woman is used to having blood drawn. The first trimester screening alone will drain you of at least seven vials, so anything after that is kid stuff.

For the GTT, you must first set aside one hour to ninety minutes of your day. Leave the house with an empty bladder because as you sign in to the lab, you will be given a 50 ml bottle of liquid. This usually comes in orange flavor, although I hear other flavors are out there. It is a flat orange soda with a subtle Gatorade top note. I was given a shot glass–size paper cup with my bottle. The receptionist said to me, "Okay, so you have to drink this entire bottle in five minutes or less."

I'm sorry, I was unaware that a dare was included in this screening.

I take a seat among the other patients waiting for bloodwork, and immediately I feel like all eyes are on me, the big pregnant lady who is about to chug a bottle of orange syrup. The bottle fills the shot glass three times. I drink all of it in under three minutes because my desire to get out of there far outweighs my fear of throwing up this stuff.

I return the empty bottle to the receptionist who notes the time. I sit down and begin the wait. I have to tell her when fifty-seven minutes have elapsed. I read, I tweet, and then the baby gets the hiccups; so I pretend that my stomach is not having visible, violent spasms. Ten minutes into the wait, the nausea finally kicks in because there is not enough room for 50 ml of orange syrup and the baby. My mantra is "stay down, stay down, stay down."

At the fifty-six-minute mark, I return to the receptionist and tell her that it's been an hour. I'm directed to the back of the lab where a tech draws three large vials of blood, and finally I'm allowed to leave.

The waiting truly begins. If the results indicate gestational diabetes, I must return for an extended GTT. I get to drink the elixir again and wait for six hours. Then I get to wait for the results of that lab work. If your test comes back positive for high glucose, then you have to take a six-hour version of this test where you drink the syrup and return six hours later to have your blood drawn. It should be called the "waiting tolerance test."

27

Please, Don't Tell Me to Relax

Relax—when used as a command, this word can make me totally incensed. At work, I have had students dare to say it to me when they think they do not deserve to face consequences for irresponsible actions. It's completely disrespectful.

I have had arguments with people, and it has been said. I'm sure I have said it to people too. I try to avoid it because I know how much I don't like to hear it. So what's my problem with it?

When you tell someone to relax, it is as if you are tuning them out. At this point, the other person may be a little worked up, but that's because they probably need to be heard and acknowledged and feel like that isn't happening. *Relax*, as a command, is condescending. It's telling the person that what he or she is saying and feeling needs to be shut off immediately. It would be much more effective as "may we please discuss this calmly?"

Now that I am pregnant, I can't stand it. Any time I remotely show emotion, my husband will tell me to relax. In a recent conversation with my mom, all she kept saying was, "Don't get upset, relax. Relax, you're pregnant," as she told me the latest family news. I know how stress can affect a fetus. I remember the public service announcements. I know in these instances it is said out of concern, but it is also said when I show the slightest bit of emotion.

I know they are saying this out of concern, but I was not able to successfully explain to Jamie how much it bothered me until I asked him, "Why is it better for me to bottle up my frustration rather than express it?" I can't shut off my emotions just because I'm pregnant.

He said, "You're right, that wouldn't be fair." It was a triumph in the battle against *relax*.

The constant reminder to relax reminds me of S. Weir Mitchell's rest cure in the nineteenth century. It was a primitive method to treat what would now be considered postpartum depression by isolating women and forcing them to do nothing except lay in bed for months and avoid excitement. By the end of the rest period, the woman would resemble a toddler, complete with round belly and uncoordinated muscle movement. Read Gilman's *The Yellow Wallpaper* to find out how it drove one woman totally insane.

I wonder if anyone ever told her to relax.

Why can't pregnant women show emotion? Is the ability to feel anger and frustration supposed to dissipate upon conception? Am I supposed to be some all-forgiving sacred vessel because I conceived? Granted, being pregnant is not an excuse to act like an emotional psychopath. I have known a few women who went off the deep end during pregnancy and were never able to return to calmer waters, but there needs to be a balance. There needs to be a time to vent and get your frustration out. There needs to be an opportunity for everyone to argue and constructively discuss frustrating situations, but freaking out or trying to anticipate and prevent someone from showing emotion is not fair. Pregnant or not, it's a difficult line to tow.

28

Ten Weeks and Counting Down

Ten weeks to go—I could buy one of those baby countdown clocks that look like an egg timer. After the first trimester screening, Jamie and I bought a twelve-month dry-erase calendar. We marked off every home improvement and reorganization project to accomplish before July.

I'm going to the doctor every two weeks now. Soon these will become weekly visits in the home stretch. What seemed like an eternity in January is rapidly approaching single-digit weeks.

As the weeks until the birth of my baby dwindle, I can't help but think about how many women die in childbirth. While these numbers have decreased in the last century, there is still always that possibility that things can go terribly wrong. According to research, the US is ranked very highly for death during childbirth, particularly for women of color. Yes, we are talking about the twenty-first century.

Think about how it must have been hundreds of years ago. Getting pregnant must have felt like a potential death sentence. Great, you're pregnant! Now, you have nine months to play Russian roulette with your life. Even if most women survived the childbirth aspect, the risk of infection after the birth was also tremendously high. Then there is the risk of the baby dying. Even if a woman and the baby made it completely through the process, families had so many kids that within a few months, a woman could be going through this again.

How could childbirth not have felt like a death sentence?

Let's not forget the fact that until approximately 1950, most women had babies at home without any painkillers. In the early fifties, doctors started performing more C-sections. Women would be knocked out for the duration of the labor. They would wake up with no memory of the birth at all.

In the 1970s, Lamaze was the natural woman's painkiller. If you were not the natural type, there were epidurals and nitrous oxide masks. The mask was given to you before the epidural could be administered. It was wrapped around your wrist. If a woman had a contraction that was too painful, all you had to do was get the mask up to your face and inhale. You would fall asleep for the duration of the contraction, that sounds like good stuff. For the record, I was delivered with lots of drugs, and I'm a rather clever woman. I don't think much damage was done.

According to Epigee.com, nitrous oxide masks are still used today in some hospitals as a means of pain relief during contractions:

> Nitrous Oxide is a great choice for women who want to take the edge off of their contractions, but who don't want a larger intervention such as an epidural. The gas takes effect quickly and wears off quickly. It is not known to have any large effect on the baby, although it does pass over the placenta while you are using it during labor.

"Pass over" or "through the placenta" means that the baby is exposed to the drugs in utero.

There are women who want to have babies naturally, with Lamaze, or in a swimming pool. There's no glory in suffering through childbirth. It does not make you a better person or a stronger woman. If you watch reality TV that focuses on pregnancy, so many women say, "I want to really experience the birth and have control over it without drugs." Translation: "I want to feel every inch of my nether regions get torn apart." Don't you think that if, sixty years ago, painless childbirth was advertised as much as painless dentistry was, women would have lined up for it? Do you go to the dentist and say, "I want control over my root canal"? I'm only going back sixty years for that point, but I think I could take it back much further.

Nine months of pregnancy is a real enough experience for me. I have watched my body take on a mind of its own. When it comes time to deliver, I'm letting the drugs take control. I don't need to scream like a cavewoman to understand that I'm giving birth. Give me an epidural and let's keep this civilized.

29

Maternity Leave

When you decide to have kids, there's a lot of counting involved. There are menstrual cycles, weeks, and trimesters to track. If you work, there's also maternity leave, family leave, and disability leave. At seven weeks pregnant, when I first saw the heartbeat flicker on the ultrasound screen, I knew that taking time off from work was in the near future. By the time we made it through the first trimester screening, I was counting down the days until maternity leave.

I plan everything. Before I was even pregnant, I knew how much time I was able to take off from work. As a tenured teacher, I do have the ability to take a year off from work (unpaid). No matter what, I knew there would be a financial sacrifice involved but one that I am willing to take. The legwork to prepare for another teacher to take my place has felt like an insurmountable task.

However, maternity leave also brings with it a few wonderful opportunities. There's the time I can spend with my baby. Also, there's an opportunity to refuel professionally and try new projects that would otherwise put off. I'm going to have my hands full. However, if I can juggle a home, family of four, and six pets, with three jobs (two part-time and one full-time), I should have a little more free time now that my full-time job is on hold.

Could maternity leave also be a rebirth of my career goals? I can try.

30

A Reflection on Maternity Leave

As a tenured public school teacher, I had the option of taking the year off without pay for which my husband and I planned. I jumped on the opportunity. I thoroughly enjoy maternity leave, although it is the most work I have ever done in my life. There is no break. It really is easier to work than to stay home with a baby, but it is remarkably rewarding at the same time.

I appreciate day care centers. I don't judge anyone who puts his or her child in day care. In most cases, it is just a necessity—especially in this country where we do not help new mothers as we should.

Many women fear that staying home will make them lose their identities. I don't believe it. Your identity gets lost if you let it. You can be you with a baby. You can stay at home with a baby too.

In my opinion, I am not comfortable with putting a newborn in daycare. When my child can communicate, I will send them to daycare, even if I am still working from home as a stay at home parent. Little ones need social interaction with other children. Don't feel guilty—just make sure you inspect every inch of the day care center you choose. Make sure they let you. Some day care centers even have video cameras that livestream to the internet so you can watch your baby from work. Ask other mothers in your area. Use the internet to research the hell out of it.

Conversely, staying home lets you see every single development as it unfolds with your newborn. Every time they discover something new, you are there. However, you are not hovering over the baby every minute of the day. With stay-at-home moms, it is very important to teach your baby how to be independent and play independently. Put the baby down. Don't carry him or her all over the place. Let them watch you work. Talk to the baby. Don't be afraid to leave the room for a few minutes. As a freelance writer, I work from home. So my child's ability to play independently is what allows me to get work done.

Also, it is absolutely necessary to get out of the house with the baby and meet other babies and moms. So definitely find a Gymboree class in your area. Also, check your local library for baby story programs. These are usually free and run by local mom groups.

31

Strange Baby Questions

I have quickly learned that when you are pregnant, there are a few questions you have to field regularly. "What gender is it?" and "What names have you picked out" are two of the most asked. When I am asked either of these questions, my usual answer is "I don't know." After all, how can I name a person I haven't seen? A name is for life, and while I may be toying with a few names, there is always the paranoid fear of giving away your top baby name or fielding a range of criticism. I have decided to forgo all this awkwardness and put naming out of my mind.

"Aren't you getting rid of your pets?" This question is one of the most bizarre. I am surprised at how often it is posed to me. I have three dogs, two birds, and a cat. They are all staying. Then I get, "But aren't you afraid of the dogs around the baby?" Why? They aren't feral. It's not like I live with a pack of wolves. I have always had pets. I think there is no better experience than a child being raised with pets. It teaches a level of sensitivity and responsibility that enriches them for life. The idea that people could be so quick to get rid of their pets bothers me. If you can't commit to a pet, how can you commit to a kid?

I was prepared for the questions about hospitals, breastfeeding, and working. But even at seven months, people are still surprising me.

Here is a list of questions I would like to ask the nonpregnant world but refrain from:

- Do you really like your hair that way?
- Why did you think that joke was funny?
- Why don't you tell the truth for a change?

See, these questions are a bit off-putting, aren't they? They are most successful in sending the same kind of feeling that I get when people ask me if I'm going to give away my dogs.

32

The Baby Shower

It is in the best taste to have your baby shower around the seventh month. You are still small enough to move around and enjoy it. The ninth month is cutting it too close to the due date. Schedule your baby shower between the end of the sixth month and beginning of the eighth. Some cultures wait until after the baby is born. I think this works well too.

I planned my own baby shower for the end of my seventh month. My husband was the host. At first, I thought I was being a control freak for throwing my own shower, but I have come to learn that it's really more common than you may imagine. The baby websites who tell you it is not appropriate for the mother to be or the couple to be to plan the shower are dream worlds. If you come from any kind of blended family, planning a shower or wedding can be like strategizing for a war.

This might be one of those times when surprises are out of the question. If you have people in your family who do not get along or who run the risk of not being entirely appropriate at social functions, then surprise parties are not for you.

Not since my wedding or bridal shower have I been this stressed out about planning an event. Once Jamie and I agreed that a surprise was out of the question, we set about planning an event where everyone would be comfortable and have a good time.

Of course, this is not always possible. Someone will always complain. Someone will always ignore the RSVP, but at the end of the day, I have to know that I tried my best.

In the end, be prepared for party planning and for lots of people touching you. The baby may be the center of attention, but that means you are too—at your biggest, puffiest, most unattractive point in your life.

As with any party, start with your guest list. Figure out how many people you are inviting. Then find a venue that can accommodate them. If you have a particular theme in mind or culture, let that be your guide. Do not have the shower at your house. It is far too much work, especially when you are nesting.

My best advice for any shower or function is to (1) put someone in charge of moving things along, have a time for when you want things to happen at the event; and (2) have something for your guests to do—you don't have to bombard them with games and activities, but there is nothing worse than going to a shower and just sitting there waiting for the guest of honor to open her gifts. A simple activity can also serve as a conversation starter for your guests to get to know other people.

Although I did have a game at my shower, I also put a pregnancy advice card at every place setting. The card asks each guest to offer a piece of advice for the mom-to-be. Many of my guests complimented these cards and appreciated the opportunity to reflect on being a mother. After the shower they were fun to read and they continue to be extremely helpful. Consider putting them into an album for easy reference and a fun keepsake. Finally, enlist a few people to help you bring your gifts home and put them away.

33

Packing for the Hospital

What's scarier, packing for the hospital or having every baby book and website tell you to pack before eighth month? I have been very fortunate in that I have never had to stay overnight in a hospital. I have never had major surgery. Outside of about three trips to the emergency room, my life is rather hospital free. The unfortunate side of this is that I am completely unprepared to stay in a hospital as a patient.

Additionally, I must pack for this hospital stay as though I were going away for the weekend. Thanks to friends and websites, I have an extensive list of things I must bring with me, a list that I am following to the letter. I hate being uncomfortable and unprepared. I have to plan for the care of pets, my house, and I have to pack clothes for the baby. Do hospitals have a bring your own onesie policy? I don't know. Do I need to bring the diaper bag? Do I need the car seat or the entire travel system? I'm going in as one person and leaving as two. This means that I have to pack for someone who isn't even here yet. What if they are unhappy with my choices?

Finally, I am told that I must pack copies of my birth plan. Here's the plan—doctors, nurses, husbands, and drugs. Those are the only people and things I want in the room with me. I'm thinking about having a "no cell phone" rule as well because there is the chance that my husband may tweet through the birth. Not to come across as inconsiderate, but I really don't see myself being receptive to phone calls or updating my Facebook status.

I know, when it's all over, "I get a baby." But that's the reason I'm going through all this in the first place—that's the catalyst, not the door prize. I think I am becoming more skeptical as the ninth month approaches.

34

A Reflection on Packing for the Hospital

Prior to giving birth, a few of my friends gave me lists of suggested items to bring to the hospital. I followed these to the letter. Once I was at the hospital, I realized that I needed to revise that list a bit.

Will the baby's father be sleeping at the hospital too? If so, you will have to pack for him. Because roaming the halls of the maternity ward in your undies is frowned upon.

I was induced. Jamie stayed with me the night of the induction. I was in the hospital for two nights after that. He slept at home. He stayed as late as he wanted. He would always return in the morning with coffee, which was very important to me.

In her books, Tracy Hogg suggests that you do not overpack for the hospital because you have to unpack it all when you get home. I agree. Here is my list of recommended hospital items:

- Two sets of pajamas, a pair of slippers, and a robe
- Underwear
- Advil and prescription meds
- Water to drink
- Snacks and hard candies
- Toiletries for showering and grooming
- Baby clothes and homecoming necessities (have dad bring the baby seat on the day you are set to go home)
- My Best Friend Pillow—remember, it helps with bottle-feeding
- Phone charger
- Clothes to wear home

- Birth plan, if you have one
- Magazine or book to read
- A bath towel for the shower—hospital towels are practically the size of a washcloth
- Flip-flops for the shower
- Travel size disinfecting wipes and Lysol
- Travel-size Lysol
- Lip balm
- Outfit for the baby
- Cash

Divide your bag into things you may need during labor and things you won't need until after. As much as I looked forward to taking a shower after I gave birth, I had a private room but no shower in the bathroom. I had to walk across the hall to a shower room in the hallway. This was a private shower in a cold, dark room with gray tile. For a woman who just had a baby, it was a most unpleasant experience.

The remainder of my hospital stay was very enjoyable. My only regret is that I did not make the most of it. I was embarrassed to lay in bed in my pajamas because I reasoned that I wasn't sick. My first, first night home, I realized just what a mistake I had made. I would have given anything for a chance to lay in that hospital bed and be cared for.

35

Cord Blood Banking

When I first heard about cord blood banking a few years ago, I thought it sounded like magic. I had no idea it was possible. One of the first decisions I ever made about having kids was that when I did, I would definitely bank the cord blood. After all, who am I to tempt fate?

There are three dominant cord blood banks. There is CBR, Cord Blood Registry; Lifebank; and Via Cord. Lifebank is located in New Jersey, as opposed to the other two that are based in Arizona and Texas.

We call them banks, but it's kind of a gruesome process to collect the cord blood. There's a kit you have to remember to bring to the hospital so that when they cut the baby's umbilical cord, they can catch the blood that pours out of this pulsing ropelike thing. The blood is then sent to the bank where stem cells are harvested from the blood and cryogenically frozen for when you need them. There is an enrollment fee and a monthly charge for this service.

Once your baby's cord blood is frozen, you will receive a certificate that tells you how many stem cells were harvested and how many are in your account. However, it does not mean that people who choose not to bank the cord blood are screwed. There is actually a public cord blood bank. Lately, companies have been fighting over patenting placenta stem cells too. But this procedure is twice the cost of cord blood.

I'm banking my baby's cord blood. This means that if he or she is faced with any life-threatening childhood illnesses like certain types of cancer, we can use the cord blood to help find a cure. If we make it through childhood without an issue, he or she will have their cord blood ready in case they sustain any damage to the central nervous system or anywhere else. Basically, this is like insurance—you hope you never have to use it.

Then there is the issue of equality. If we have another baby, we are now obligated to bank their cord blood as well. You can't save the stem cells of one kid and not the other. That would be terrible. I don't even know how many doses of cord blood you can get out of one collection. Honestly, I hope I never find out.

36

The Countdown

In case anyone out there is trying to tell themselves otherwise, the truth is that, yes, when you are nine months pregnant, everyone is staring at you. I catch people staring at me constantly—men, women, even children. I'm not even that big. Maybe I'm just saying that as a poor attempt to tell the world to go look at pregnant women larger than I. That wouldn't be right.

There are women who embrace the pregnant body. To this I say, I understand why women went into confinement. Who needs all this out in public? Moving is a struggle. I'm grateful that I don't waddle. There's swelling, shortness of breath, perspiration. There's nothing glowing and beautiful about it. That's to say nothing of the enormous breasts that impede my every movement. Oh yes, please confine me to a nice, cool room. Please. My brain is like a Slurpee, and there's nothing substantial for me to contribute to the world at this time. Usually, I can't even remember what I was saying.

Then there are the physical shortcomings. I can't reach anything. I can't lift or carry much because of the giant belly and because I can get hurt. Do I need to send myself to the hospital because I just had to carry a heavy box to the basement? When you are used to being an independent, self-sufficient woman, being pregnant is a bitch. There's a difference between asking for help and needing help. These days, I need help, and then the irony of having to ask for it kicks in. People insist on telling me, "Wow, you're getting close." Really? Am I? I hadn't noticed.

Who knows what horrible and skeptical things await after the birth.

37

The Game Plan

As it gets closer to the estimated delivery day, my house is filled with a certain sense of uncertainty. The air is full of the coming change. The change of schedule, lifestyle, responsibility—all the things you plan on sacrificing when you decide to start a family. However, you do get about nine months to say goodbye to these things. For Jamie and I, we only have freedom every other weekend and after seven on weeknights because he has two children. So we are saying goodbye to the rare time that we were a couple.

It's not a bad thing, but the change is imminent, and we are so eager to get a new lifestyle and schedule rolling that it seems like this kid will never come out! Still, there is much preparation. We have had to arrange for kid care and pet care. What I wasn't planning on was a phone chain.

Now, it's no surprise that I'm anxious. I imagine that our family is too. However, if one more person asks me to call them when I'm going to the hospital, I'm going to snap. While we do have a small list of go-to people who will need phone calls, it's safe to say that this will be one of those times in my life when I don't want to be on the phone. I'm trying to come up with ways to compromise this situation. So far, all I can think of is Facebook. Maybe this would be a good time for a status update. Something like, "Sadie's in labor, spread the word amongst yourselves. We'll call when it's over."

I don't know what's worse, having to call people or the possibility that they will continue to call me to see how things are going. We all know how this is going to end—with a baby. It's not a cliffhanger. While I'm not trying to diffuse anyone's excitement, I do want to implore their patience. Doing things delicately is not in my vocabulary when I'm nervous.

The plan is that there is no plan. There can't be. There are too many factors. There are things that will have to be put in motion and family volunteers to notify, but how much can one pregnant woman remember?

Is it over yet or is this just the beginning?

As skeptical as I am, there have been many things that I have taken for granted, particularly my ankles. They usually do a bit of a disappearing act in the early evening.

When you get to the ninth month, every day is a crap shoot. Mobility is out the window. Moving takes a tremendous amount of momentum. You begin sleeping in naps like Da Vinci but without the genius because your memory actually gets worse—ninety-minute to three-hour increments of sleep broken up by trips to the bathroom and rotating sides to sleep on like a chicken leg on a grill.

If you are due in the summer or live in a warm climate, the swelling, exacerbated by the heat, is a really lovely side effect of full-term pregnancy. Fingers, face, feet, I think my arms are swollen. I am a fluid-filled, puffy version of my former self. Now, let's go out in public so people can stare at me!

The size of my stomach is at an all-time high, as well it should be. However, it is not at that all-time low that will mark the end of this game. The weekly trips to the doctor go something like, "No change yet, but maybe we'll hear from you this week!" Or my personal favorite, "We're on vacation, try to hold out until Monday!" I feel like this child will attend college from my uterus.

Yet it isn't even close to over. As uncomfortable as I feel now, I still have to give birth. Then I get to heal and breastfeed. The pregnancy phase is ending, but I am at the threshold of the postpartum and baby phases of this process.

I try not to take it for granted. It was almost a year ago that I expressed my concerns over the possibility of even being able to conceive. I still don't get the "beautiful process" and "wonderful pregnancy" thing. It's all very oxymoronic.

Have I mentioned that I am in a positively delightful mood?

38

Giving Birth

There are a few possible scenarios to giving birth.

Scenario 1. "Oh, my water broke!" This means that you have made it to your due date—give or take, a few days before or after—but your membranes have ruptured on their own. Yes, there is a lot of fluid. It should be clear. If it is tinged brown or green, this is meconium. It means that the baby has had a bowel movement in utero. The doctors must be quick to clean out the baby's mouth and nose so that it doesn't aspirate the meconium. Otherwise, it's not the end of the world, but it can put your baby at a higher risk for pneumonia if it is aspirated.

In any event, your water has broken. You go to the hospital or birthing center. You make your pain relief choices, (more on that later). You are in labor.

Chances are, you feel like someone is grabbing your hip bones and yanking down as hard as possible in an attempt to rip your body at the waist. Meanwhile, fluid is shooting out of your vagina. This is called a contraction, and they go from bad to worse. Yes, I know what you're thinking: *Breathe! Breathe! Pant! Blow!* Bullshit. It's all bullshit. The breathing is an attempt to distract you from the pain. It hurts. It's the kind of pain that your body blocks out after you give birth because of the shock. Good luck with that.

Scenario 2. "I'm having contractions!" Great! Chances are, the baby has moved down in the pelvis. You are effacing, and pretty soon your water will break. But then again, it may not. Most likely, you will time the contractions. (Most phones even have an app for that.) You may have real contractions and go to the hospital, but most women must have their water broken when they get there. Breaking the water (rupturing the membrane) helps to move labor along. So if you are having contractions but maybe you are not dilating quickly or your labor has slowed down, breaking the water will move things along again!

39

So You've Missed Your Due Date

If there are no signs of labor after your doctor performs a nonstress test, chances are, you will be induced.

An induction is when labor is deliberately brought on. First, you are given Cervidil to "ripen" (gross) your cervix. This hormone is implanted into your cervix, and it's supposed to make the cervix become soft and shift positions. Essentially, your cervix has to move down to meet your vagina and ultimately create a chute. I didn't know this until a resident explained it to me at the hospital.

Everything is done to make you dilate. Once the Cervidil does its job, you will most likely get Pitocin. This is another hormone type of drug that brings on contractions. After some time on Pitocin, your doctor will break your water because it rarely breaks on its own, especially during an induction. Now, you are in pain. Your body feels like someone has their hands around your hip bones and is tugging with all their might to sever you at the waist. Those are contractions, and they suck.

If you are offered an epidural, take it. The sting of the novocaine in your back pales in comparison to how effectively the pain relief works. After the epidural, you'll get a catheter. I was terrified of getting a catheter, but I never felt it go in or come out. It was nice to not have to get up to go to the bathroom. An empty bladder helps the labor to progress. When you are finally ten centimeters, the doctor will remove the catheter so it doesn't get in the way when you push.

I don't believe that you need to be able to feel pressure in order to push. It's the twenty-first century. During this entire process, you have been hooked up to a fetal monitor. It tracks your contractions and the baby's heart rate. You can watch the contractions on the screen and know exactly when to push. It works. I felt nothing.

Here's my best advice: try to stay in shape because it will take less time to push the kid out. After eighteen hours of labor and drugs, I was not going to spend hours pushing. I was thankful for every minute of yoga and power walking that I have ever done, and I hate exercise. I delivered within thirty minutes, and I didn't feel any of it.

40

After You Give Birth

Once the baby is born, you're not as preoccupied with what is going on with your body. The baby is cleaned up, and you hold him or her. You will have to deliver the afterbirth, but you will be so pleasantly distracted that it probably won't bother you.

Let's talk about the undercarriage. It's been through a lot. Some women like to watch the horror. Some women will even look in a mirror; people take pictures or video. Jamie was on strict orders to do no such thing. The only birth I've ever seen is on YouTube.

While you're admiring your baby, your doctor is repairing your nether regions. The area around your vagina may have torn or you may have received an episiotomy. Many doctors today are holding off on cutting and letting their patients tear naturally. According to BabiesOnline.com,

> *If you are planning on a vaginal birth, whether or not to have an episiotomy is an important decision to consider. While all women know that childbirth is painful, the thought of having her vaginal area cut or torn is very frightening. It is best to know all the options available before labor begins, so that your birth plan expresses your specific wishes.*
>
> **Episiotomies**
> *Are episiotomies necessary? Many women today say no. Episiotomies used to be done routinely during a vaginal childbirth by the doctor or midwife as a way to help the woman avoid getting a tear.*

There are two main types of episiotomies – the midline and the mediolateral. The midline is when the doctor makes the incision straight down towards the anus, and the mediolateral is an incision made diagonally to help avoid a later tear into the anal area.

Episiotomies are said to have both positive and negative aspects

The benefits can include:
- Faster birth
- Prevention of tearing
- Protection against incontinence
- Protection against pelvic floor relaxation
- Faster rate of healing than tears

The negative aspects can include:
- Infection
- Increased pain
- An increase in 3rd and 4th degree vaginal lacerations (euphemistically called extensions)
- Longer healing times
- Increased discomfort when intercourse is resumed

Many midwives believe that there are better ways to avoid a tear than getting an episiotomy. These might include:
- Good nutrition (healthy skin stretches more easily)
- Kegels (exercise for your pelvic floor muscles)
- Prenatal discussion with your care provider about episiotomy
- Prenatal perineal massage
- A slowed second stage (controlled pushing)
- Warm compresses, perineal massage and support during delivery

Tearing

Many organizations that do not consider episiotomies as necessary believe that it is better for a woman to tear, but is it really? Some make the argument that not every woman will tear, and that those that do may only tear a tiny bit, *resulting in only one or two stitches, vs. the 10, 20 or even more needed with an episiotomy. Not every woman will tear during delivery, and so some women may have episiotomies unnecessarily.*

There is a negative side to allowing your body to tear naturally as well. Both episiotomies and tears are considered by degrees. The most common is the second degree tear or cut, which extends halfway back to the woman's anus. The least common, but most painful, is the fourth

Both options today are acceptable in the medical field, and episiotomies are actually done less routinely than they used to be on pregnant women. It is best for a woman to research both options before she goes into labor so that she can choose which one she prefers while writing out her birth plan, and talking to the doctor at delivery.

For example, my doctors were in favor of tearing because sometimes doctors are scissor happy with episiotomies and cut you more than necessary. It didn't hurt immediately after the birth, but it took about seven weeks before I was not aware of my lady parts.

You will be painfully aware. If you thought there was a lot going on during the birth, what with blood and fluid shooting out of you, just wait. After you give birth, you have to deal with bleeding healing. There may be stitches dissolving. Your vagina has been through a very traumatic experience.

If you are not given cold compresses, ask for them. I was given an ice pack that looked like a giant sanitary napkin. As bulky and intimidating as it looked, it was amazing relief.

Also be prepared for nurses to check you. They check to see how much you are bleeding. I guess it's better that they do check than ignore it. If you have any questions about anything you are feeling, make sure you tell the doctors and nurses immediately.

Also, continue to rest when you get home. Just because you are being released doesn't mean you are better. Make sure you have people around to help you with the baby—the dad, especially. It's just as important for him to learn the ropes.

C-section

If you need a Cesarean, you are facing a major surgical procedure. There's nothing you did wrong. It's just the course your journey took. You will be given anesthesia to numb you from upper back down. A horizontal incision will be made across your abdomen. This also breaks the amniotic sack in the process. The abdomen is stretched open, the baby removed and sack removed, and then everything is sewn up. This usually means there is internal scarring in the uterus. Once you have had a C-section, you will probably have Cesarean for other births unless you can find a doctor to perform VBAC (vaginal birth after Cesarean).

Unfortunately, you will not be able to hold your baby immediately after they are born, but you will make contact with your baby. It will take longer to heal from a C-section, and your mobility will be limited after birth, more so than with a vaginal delivery.

41

I'm Not Depressed—I'm Stressed

Having a baby is stressful. For a while I thought I was depressed. So I did what any good neurotic person does—I Googled. I Googled "postpartum depression." The results said, "Postpartum depression is depression that occurs soon after having a baby. Some health professionals call it postpartum nonpsychotic depression," and took as many online quizzes and evaluations as I could. Nothing. I did not seem to have any of the symptoms of postpartum depression, postpartum mood disorder, or whatever else it is called now. Then I happened upon the term *postpartum stress*. This seemed to make much more sense.

Not leaving anything to chance, I found a therapist who confirmed that having a baby is a very stressful experience.

Think about it—our culture is crazy. We spend so much time planning for a baby, but we never really stop to think about how we will actually handle and feel during this core-shaking life change.

Stressed, I was.

After talking to a professional, I really feel so much more relieved that I can identify the stress. I can name it and call myself out when I feel it. And it's okay.

Why isn't this in the baby books? Why do we jump from getting pregnant to postpartum depression? Why don't we just stop to admit that having a baby will scare the crap out of the most stable person. In the hospital, it is required that a new mother is screened for postpartum depression twice (or each day that you are in the hospital). During these depression screenings, I was never asked about stress.

The moment this creature starts crying inconsolably, you feel their hot little breath in your face and the bottle can't heat up fast enough—it's stressful; it can be downright traumatic.

I'm lucky I have a husband who helps. I can say, "I need a break, you have to take her." I know there are many women out there who are alone—or, worse, they have a nonresponsive spouse.

Did you know that many parents of premature babies will later on suffer from symptoms of post-traumatic Stress disorder? How's that for stress?

It's almost unfair. In the hospital, you really can't grasp how much things are about to change. It would be much better if a nurse came to your home and gave you this screening a few days after you leave the hospital.

The bottom line is that I owe it to my daughter to learn how to manage my stress. Motherhood is isolating and frustrating. It dismantles your life and rebuilds it. No matter how much you nest, you're never prepared. Stress comes with the territory.

42

Parenting for the Skeptical Woman: The First Ten Years

Violet Antonia Laurens was born on July 26, 2010, at 4:35 p.m. She was eight pounds, three ounces; twenty-one inches long; and full of personality. She continues to keep me skeptical and changes my world on a regular basis. Keeping a blog throughout my pregnancy really gave me the opportunity to reflect on the different experiences and waves of emotion that I weathered over the last year. I was tired, emotional, puffy, uncomfortable, and perpetually curious about what was going to happen when I became a mother. One of the first things is, I never expected her to be so attached to me. I know it sounds crazy, but I just did not give myself the credit.

Here are other things I did not expect:

1. Being protective. I do want my child to be able to go to other family members. I do not want her to be afraid of people. At the same time, I wonder if she feels abandoned when she does this. Also, I do not like having her around people whom I don't like. While these situations are rare, they make the protective instinct soar.
2. I had to realize that she is an actual person with her own personality, likes, and dislikes. I actually had to get to know her. I have heard other women question whether or not they will love their babies because they don't know them. The way I see it is that she had nine months to get to know me. She had no choice. She ate what I ate, she went where

I went. I really had no idea what she was like at all. What I do know about her is that she is half me. So that's a good place to start. Ten years later, there are so many pieces of her personality that I observed when she was a baby that I still see today.

For example when I was induced, she was not ready to be born. When she was born, she came out crying and pouting as if she truly disapproved of this barbaric experience. Since then, she has done everything exactly when she is ready. It has nothing to do with me or with baby milestones—it's all her own pace. She hates to feel rushed.

3. I did not anticipate giving birth a week late and having to evict her.
4. I didn't think that being home would be nearly as enjoyable as it is. I have never had so many women, with grown children, tell me that I should stay home because they regret going back to work when they should have made the sacrifice to stay home. This one really rattles me. These women know far more than I do. All I know is that the last two months have flown by. Every Sunday, I think about the Sunday night when I was induced. I look at all the pictures I take and marvel at how much she is changing and how much she has changed me. I returned to work, outside the home, when she was eighteen months old. By the time she was two, she was definitely ready for nursery school. In fact, she thrived.
5. I didn't expect her to make me want to change my life. Think about it—how do you want your children to remember you? I don't want my daughter to say, "I remember my mother being tired, high-strung, and stressed out." Doesn't "my mom is a happy and confident person" sound so much better? When people say that having a child changes you, it seems cliché, but it sort of does. I think you can accept, reject, or ignore the change. But it certainly makes you reflect on who you are even the most skeptical of us.

Here's the table of contents of my upcoming book *Parenting for the Skeptical Woman: Ten Years Later*:

- Chapter 1: Bonding
- Chapter 2: Childcare
- Chapter 3: Feed Your Skeptical Child
- Chapter 4: Sleep
- Chapter 5: Potty Training: Inconvenient Pooping
- Chapter 6: Communicating
- Chapter 7: Clothing
- Chapter 8: Kid Gear
- Chapter 9: Vominiting
- Chapter 10: Socialization
- Chapter 11: All Things Unexpected

REFERENCES

Ballard, Jeanne L., Christine E. Auer, and Jane C. Khoury. "Ankyloglossia: Assessment, Incidence, and Effect of Frenuloplasty on the Breastfeeding Dyad." *Pediatrics* 110, no. 5 (November 1, 2002). https://doi.org/10.1542/peds.110.5.e63.

Dansinger, Michael. "Oral Glucose Tolerance Test for Gestational & Type 2 Diabetes." WebMD. WebMD, November 14, 2018. http://www.webmd.com/baby/oral-glucose-tolerance-test.

Dryden-Edwards, Roxanne. "Postpartum Depression Screening, Symptoms & Treatment." eMedicineHealth. eMedicineHealth, February 1, 2019. http://www.emedicinehealth.com/postpartum_depression/article_em.htm.

"Expert Info for Pregnancy & Parenting." BabyCenter. Accessed October 30, 2020. http://www.babycenter.com/.

"The First Trimester Ultrasound (NT) Scan." Baby2See. Accessed October 30, 2020. http://www.baby2see.com/medical/nuchal_12weekscan.html/.

Missing Angel. Accessed October 30, 2020. http://www.missingangel.org/.

"Laughing Your Way Through Labor." Epigee.org. Accessed October 30, 2020. http://www.epigee.org/nitrous-oxide-for-labor.html.

"Maternity Fashion & Basics Online at Motherhood.com." Motherhood Maternity. Accessed October 30, 2020. http://www.destinationmaternity.com/.

Motherhood Maternity. Accessed October 30, 2020. http://www.destinationmaternity.com/.

Parenting Weekly. Accessed October 30, 2020. http://www.parentingweekly.com/pregnancy/pregnancy-symptoms/linea-negra.htm.

"Pregnancy and Baby Information - Conceive Fetus Pregnant Labor Birth Timeline." Baby2See. Accessed October 30, 2020. http://www.baby2see.com.

"Prenatal Tests." American Pregnancy Association, October 1, 2020. http://www.americanpregnancy.org/prenataltesting/quadscreen.html.

Shiel Jr., William C. "Medical Definition of Relaxin." MedicineNet. MedicineNet, January 25, 2017. http://www.medterms.com/script/main/art.asp?articlekey=13411.

"Spina Bifida." Mayo Clinic. Mayo Foundation for Medical Education and Research, December 17, 2019. http://www.mayoclinic.com/health/spina-bifida/DS00417/DSECTION=preparing-for-your-appointment.

Target Corporate Website. Target Corporation. Accessed October 30, 2020. http://www.target.com.

"Thalassemia." Mayo Clinic. Mayo Foundation for Medical Education and Research, November 22, 2019. http://www.mayoclinic.com/health/thalassemia/DS00905.

TheBump.com, n.d. www.thebump.com.

"Trisomy." Wikipedia. Wikimedia Foundation, August 21, 2020. http://en.wikipedia.org/wiki/Trisomy.
http://www.babiesonline.com/articles/pregnancy/episiotomyvstearing.asp

www.ingramcontent.com/pod-product-compliance
Lightning Source LLC
Chambersburg PA
CBHW021448070526
44577CB00002B/309